CROCHET
FOR A BEAUTIFUL
HOME

CROCHET
FOR A BEAUTIFUL HOME

Sedgewood® Press

Published by Sedgewood® Press

For Sedgewood® Press
Director Elizabeth P. Rice
Editorial Project Manager
Bruce B. Macomber
Production Manager Bill Rose

Produced for Sedgewood® Press by
Marshall Cavendish Books Limited
58 Old Compton Street
London W1V 5PA

For Marshall Cavendish
House Editor Dorothea Hall
Editor Elizabeth Floyd
Designer Trevor Vertigan
Production Manager Richard Churchill

First Printing 1987

© Marshall Cavendish Limited 1987
Distributed by
Meredith Corporation

ISBN 0-696-02307-5
Library of Congress Catalog Card
Number 87-060242

Printed in
the United States of America

10 9 8 7 6 5 4 3

Contents

Introduction

A delicate handmade tablecloth, a colorful afghan, or lace-trimmed guest towels — these enhance and personalize any home and make its owners proud. They are more costly to buy than most of us can afford or justify. But we can have them, nevertheless — and in many cases quite easily — by making them ourselves in crochet. This book aims to help you design and crochet beautiful things for your home or to give as very special gifts.

Crochet is a popular art not only because it produces a wide variety of beautiful fabrics for many different uses, but also because it requires very little in the way of equipment. All you need is a hook and some kind of thread — anything from string, straw or strips of gingham to silk, angora wool or ribbon. Crochet can be worked in rounds or in rows to any shape or size in a vast number of patterns using a few basic stitches. Large items such as bedspreads can be made in small pieces, usually circles, squares or octagons, which can be carried easily and worked on in spare moments. These pieces can then be sewn together in patterns to form lace, Aran patchwork and many fabrics in between.

Crochet for a beautiful home is designed not only to give you beautiful patterns to follow, but also to give you ideas for creating your own designs. Many of the patterns have alternative stitch designs. You can also substitute different colors or threads. Or you can expand a tray cloth pattern to make a lacy bedspread, enlarge a coaster to make a place mat or trim a linen dresser scarf with a pretty edging used on sheets or towels.

Each chapter focuses on a different type of household accessory. These include afghans, pillows, table linens, bed and bath accessories, rugs and curtains and finishing touches — unusual items for your home or items not usually crocheted such as trim for lampshades, a bunch of bright flowers and a hammock. To give you some idea of the flexibility of crochet, we have used different techniques within each chapter to show different ways of making one type of item such as an afghan. We have also used the same technique, such as filet crochet, in different chapters to show that one technique can be used to make several different items such as curtains and bedspreads.

Household accessories are a good place for beginners to start in crochet because most require little or no shaping and fit may not be critical. *Getting Started* provides basic information for those who are new to crochet and eager to begin. There are sections on tools and equipment, on how to read patterns including those written in symbols, on gauge and on finishing. The last section in the book, *Basic Skills*, shows in clear illustrations and directions how to do the basic stitches and techniques.

For experienced crocheters, the sky is the limit. You can start immediately on one of the more intricate patterns using the *Basic Skills* section as a refresher on some of the stitches and techniques if needed. Or you can create your own designs using the hints on design in *Getting Started*.

Beginners or experienced, all crocheters can use this book to make beautiful things for your homes or those of your friends. Start now, work at your leisure and enjoy the results forever.

Getting started

A hook, some thread and a pattern and you are on your way to making beautiful accessories for your home. Here the wide range of hooks and threads available is discussed. Information on how to read and understand patterns and how to achieve a professional finish through gauge, seaming and blocking is also given. For those who want to go beyond the patterns, there is a section on creating your own originals.

Tools and Materials

The only essential tool required for crochet is a hook. Hooks come in a wide range of sizes suitable for different types of thread. For fine threads in cotton or silk, there are steel hooks ranging from size 14 steel, the smallest, to size 0, the largest. Steel hooks are generally used to make delicate edgings, lacy tablecloths and other fine work.

The middle range of hooks, the ones used most frequently, are made of aluminum or plastic and come in size from B, the smallest, to K, the largest. These hooks may also be identified by numbers starting with 1, the equivalent of B. Medium-sized hooks are generally used with cotton or wool yarn to make such items as afghans, pillow covers and bath mats.

The largest hooks are made of wood and range in size from 10, the smallest, to 16, the largest. These jumbo hooks are used with bulky yarn, jute or strips of fabric to make mats and rugs. Some of the largest of these, called jiffy hooks, are made in plastic. For a complete list of hook sizes with their metric equivalents, see the chart on page 11.

Special hooks for Tunisian crochet and hairpin lace crochet are also available but are not used in any of the projects in this book.

The range of materials that can be used with a crochet hook to make a fabric is almost endless. It includes leather thongs, rafia, string, ribbon, macramé cord, strips of fabric, braid, embroidery thread, wire and ribbon.

Most people, however, use the threads and yarns that are packaged and sold as knitting or crochet yarn. Most of these are made of various natural and synthetic fibers that are spun to produce long threads of varying thicknesses and textures. It is this threadlike quality plus the pliability of yarn that makes it suitable for looping into stitches.

One of the fibers widely used to crochet home accessories is cotton. Crochet cotton comes in a wide range of weights or thicknesses which are graded by number — the larger the number, the finer the thread. Some of the cotton threads available include Speed cro-sheen (size 3) and pearl cotton (size 5) which are fairly thick cottons that come in a wide range of colors, six-cord cottons (sizes 20 and 30) which are medium threads that come in white and ecru and in some cases in colors, and tatting cotton (size 70), a fine thread that comes in a number of colors. Cotton threads are usually mercerized, a process that gives them strength and sheen. They may also be "boilfast" which means that they are colorfast. Many cotton threads are sold by length rather than by weight. See Working in fine cotton on page 14.

Wool and synthetic wool-like yarns or combinations of both come in a vast range that has been growing even larger in recent years with the introduction of many novelty yarns and the importation of yarns from Europe and Japan. American yarns come in a number of standard weights. These include:

a fingering — a fine yarn which makes a lacy or delicate fabric

b baby yarn — a lightweight yarn that comes in many pastel colors

c sport or sport-weight yarn — a medium-weight yarn that can be used for lightweight blankets and afghans

d knitting worsted or knitting worsted weight — a heavy yarn used for warmer or heavier afghans and pillow covers

e rug and bulky yarns — a very heavy yarn used for a thick or bulky look or feel, or for extra warmth. It is often used for rugs and bath mats.

Two types of British yarn now available in the United States and

becoming more familiar to American knitters and crocheters are double knitting and four-ply. Double knitting is a smooth yarn, slightly lighter in weight than knitting worsted. The term also applies to European novelty yarns that knit to about the same gauge. Four-ply yarn is another smooth yarn; this one is slightly lighter than sport yarn. The phrase "knits as four-ply" is applied to novelty yarns that knit to the same gauge. If you decide to use these yarns instead of their American counterparts, you may have to use a larger hook to obtain the same gauge.

Threads and yarns are also available in a number of natural fibers other than cotton and wool. These include silk, a luxury yarn produced in a range of thicknesses and textures; linen, made from flax and often mixed with cotton; mohair, a fluffy goat hair yarn; angora, a delicate, soft yarn made from rabbit fur; and alpaca, a slightly hairy yarn that comes from a llama-like South American animal and is usually sold in natural colors.

Natural fibers can be, and often are, combined with such synthetics as acrylic, nylon and rayon to reduce the price of the yarn, to change its characteristics or to make the finished work easier to care for. Synthetics can be made to look like wool and, when made in standard weights, can be used interchangeably with the natural fiber yarns they imitate.

Very different from the familiar standard weights such as knitting worsted are the growing number of highly-textured novelty yarns. These include bouclé, chenille and metallic yarns. Most are made from a combination of synthetics and natural fibers. Novelty yarns can sometimes be used effectively to vary the texture of some of the pieces in simple patchwork crochet. They can also provide interesting textures in picture crochet. It is a good idea to try these yarns in the stitch and shape you have in mind before buying large quantities. In general, the more highly textured the yarn, the simpler the stitch should be. Otherwise, the stitch will be obscured by the fuzz, bumps or pile of the yarn.

It is important to check the fiber content of any yarn you plan to use in a project because it will tell you a great deal about the look and the durability of the finished work and about its care. Wool, for example, holds it shape better and stays clean longer than synthetics, but most wools must be hand washed. Synthetics, on the other hand, are usually machine washable making them a good choice for items such as baby blankets that must be washed frequently.

Most cotton threads are smooth and therefore easy to work. They dye well and are long-lasting. And if the thread or yarn has been pre-shrunk and is colorfast, items made in cotton will also usually wash well.

The best way to familiarize yourself with threads or yarns is to visit a shop that has a large selection, look at what is available and read the labels. Clerks in yarn shops can often help you select a good yarn for your project and tell you how much you will need. If you cannot get help in estimating amounts, buy one ball or skein and use it all up making a section of the item. Measure the area you have covered and then estimate what percentage of the total area your sample is. One ball will provide the same percentage of the yarn needed.

When you buy the yarn for a project, buy a little more than you think you will need for the whole job, and make sure that all the balls or skeins are from the same dye lot. The number is printed on the label. Many stores will take back any full balls or skeins that are left. If not, you can use leftover yarn to make a small mat, contrasting trim, or multicolored granny squares.

In addition to hooks and yarn, you may need a few other supplies for finishing your work. These include a ruler or tape for checking gauge (see page 12), a small pair of scissors for cutting the thread, stainless steel pins for blocking, and a tapestry needle (size 5–13) with a large eye and rounded end for sewing pieces of crochet together. You may also need an iron and ironing board for light pressing, and towels for blocking.

Understanding crochet patterns

Crochet patterns pack a maximum amount of information into a minimum amount of space by using abbreviations or symbols. These are simple and logical, once you understand them, and make following patterns easier.

Abbreviations

Many of the abbreviations used in crochet patterns such as "approx" for approximately and "cont" for continue are probably already familiar to you. Others refer to the different kinds of stitches such as "dc" for double crochet. The abbreviations used in this book are explained in the chart on page 11. Any abbreviations which are not in the chart are explained in the pattern where they are used.

(Parentheses) around several steps in a pattern mean that you should repeat these steps; you will be told how many times to repeat just beyond the closing parenthesis. Parentheses may also enclose a number of stitches to be worked into one stitch or space. Steps included between *asterisks* should be repeated continuously for as long as there are enough stitches left in the row or round to do it.

Crochet abbreviations

alt = alternate(ly)
approx = approximately
beg = begin(ning)
ch = chain(s)
cont = continu(e)(ing)
dc = double crochet
dec = decreas(e)(ing)
dtr = double triple crochet
foll = follow(s)(ing)
gr(s) = group(s)
hdc = half double crochet
in = inch(es)
inc = increas(e)(ing)
LH = left hand
pat = pattern
rem = remain(ing)
rep = repeat
RH = right hand
RS = right side
sc = single crochet
sl st = slip stitch
sp = space(s)
st(s) = stitch(es)
tog = together
tr = triple crochet
tr tr = triple triple crochet
WS = wrong side
yo = yarn over hook

Symbols and charts

Directions for crochet, especially for more intricate patterns such as lace, may be given in chart form. At first glance, charts look confusing, but actually they make the work easier because they show exactly what kind of stitch is to go where and how the pattern builds up. At the end of every row, you can compare your work with the chart to make sure you are on the right track.

The list on page 12 shows the symbols used in this book. Other patterns may use slightly different symbols so do not assume these are universal. Check the symbols on the pattern you are using.

Before using a charted pattern for the first time, practice with the sample chart on page 13. If you have difficulty, you can check with the directions that accompany the chart.

Crochet hook sizes

American	Metric	American	Metric	American	Metric
Steel				Wood	
14	0.60	B	2.50	10	—
13	—	C	3.00	11	8.00
12	0.75	D	—	12	—
11	—	E	3.50	13	9.00
10	1.00	F	4.00	15	10.00
9	—	G	4.50	16	—
8	1.25	H	5.00		
7	1.50	—	5.50		
6	—	I	6.00		
5	—	J	6.50		
4	1.75	K	7.00		
3	—				
2	—				
1	—				
0	2.00				

Note:
American hook sizes vary slightly according to the manufacturer

Following a crochet chart

Directions for crochet given in chart form are less familiar than the usual abbreviations but are easy to follow.

In addition to basic crochet stitch symbols, many crochet designers now use more complicated stitch techniques. The list given below includes both basic and all international symbols used in crochet patterns.

Practice using symbols by working the Fishbone pattern from the chart below.

In addition to the symbols follow the numbers given for each row.

If you need help, conventional row by row instructions are also provided.

Symbol	Stitch
◎	first chain
○	chain (ch)
⌢	slip stitch (sl st)
+	single crochet (sc)
T	half double crochet (hdc)
∓	double crochet (dc)
∓	triple crochet (tr)
∓	double triple crochet (dtr)
∓	triple triple crochet (tr tr)
⊥	Work stitch into front loop only
⊼	Work stitch into back loop only
+ / ○	Work under two strands of stitch
∓	Work under the chain

Symbol	Stitch
∮	Work around the stitch from the *front*
∳	Work around the stitch from the *back*
∓	Work stitch from the back of the work (*Note:* Any stitch shown in broken lines should be worked into the back of another stitch or from the back of the work.)
∓ 8	Make stitch longer than usual; make it as long as the number of chains shown at the right
4	Begin a single crochet: keep 2 loops on the hook
∮	Begin a double crochet: keep 3 loops on the hook
∮	Begin a triple crochet: keep 4 looks on the hook
∮	Begin a double triple: keep five loops on the hook

Symbol	Stitch
ℓ	Yarn over hook and draw through one loop
ℓℓ	Yarn over hook and draw through two loops
ℓℓℓ	Yarn over hook and draw through three loops, etc
⊕	Single crochet popcorn or bobble
⊕	Double crochet popcorn or bobble
⊕	Triple crochet popcorn or bobble
⊕	Double crochet puff stitch
⊕	Triple crochet puff stitch
⊕	Double crochet cluster
⊕	Triple crochet cluster
↗	Do not turn

Fishbone chart

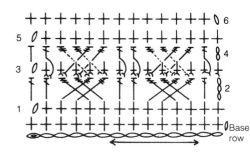

Fishbone pattern
Make a multiple of 6ch plus 3 extra.
Base row (RS) 1sc into 2nd ch from hook, 1sc into each ch to end. Turn.
1st row Ch 1, skip first sc, 1sc into each st to end. Turn.
2nd row Ch 3, skip first st, 1dc into next st, *skip 2 sts, 1 tr into each of next 2 sts, 1 tr into each of 2 sts just skipped, 1dc into each of next 2 sts, rep from * to end. Turn.

3rd row Ch 1, skip first st, working into *back* loops only, 1sc into each st to end. Turn.
4th row Ch 2, skip first st, working all sts of this row into loops of 2nd row left unworked, 1dc into next st, * skip next 2 sts, 1 tr into each of next 2 sts, working from back 1 tr into each of 2 sts just skipped, 1dc into each of next 2 sts, rep from * to end, ending with 1 hdc into turning ch. Turn.
5th and 6th rows As 1st row.

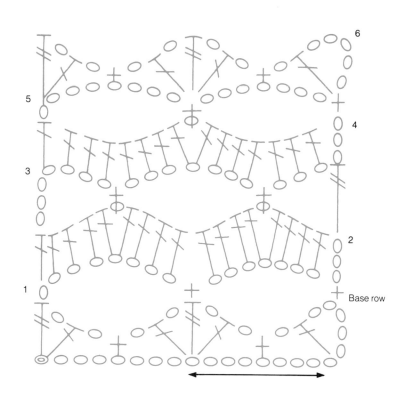

Gauge

Gauge is extremely important to the success of crochet. The gauge is given at the beginning of every pattern. It tells you the number of stitches and the number of rows you must have in a given space if your work is to look the same and be the same size as that in the photograph. If you get more stitches and rows per inch, your work will be tighter and smaller. If you get fewer stitches and rows, your work will be looser and larger. To ensure that you get the correct gauge, you must make a sample using the specified hook, yarn and stitch in the pattern and then measure the number of stitches and rows you are getting to the space given. If the recommended gauge is 20 stitches and 15 rows in a four-inch square for example, make your sample at least 26 stitches wide and six inches long so you will not have to include edge stitches and rows in your measurements (they may distort it). Lay the sample on a flat surface and mark the beginning and ending of 20 stitches and the beginning and ending of 15 rows with straight pins. Measure between the pins. Your stitches and rows should take up exactly four inches. If they take up more, try again with a smaller hook; if they take up less, try with a larger hook. You must keep trying until you get the gauge right — difficult as it is to hold back when what you really want to do is to get started.

When the gauge is given for a square or other shaped piece, make that piece using the correct stitch, yarn and hook and then measure it.

You must also make a gauge sample using the hook, yarn and stitch you intend to use when you are designing your own work. You can then either design from your own gauge or rework the sample until you get the gauge that fits your design.

Finishing

Just as important as gauge in producing beautiful results in crochet is finishing. Finishing takes time and should be done carefully.

The first step is to darn in the loose

At the end of every row simply compare your crochet with the chart.

13

ends of thread or yarn. This is more difficult in crochet than in knitting because there are usually open spaces in the work and these can become escape routes for loose ends, especially if the item is pulled or moved frequently. Darn the yarn into the backs of several stitches with one or two back stitches along the way. These should go through the yarn of the tail and split it. On some yarns, this is the only way to make loose ends reliably secure.

The next step is to block. Pin each piece to the correct size and shape on a towel over an old blanket or a board. Cover with a damp cloth or spray with water and leave until thoroughly dry. If necessary, press very lightly being careful not to flatten the stitches and destroy the texture. Do not slide the iron over the work or let its full weight rest on it.

For crochet done in one piece, blocking is the last step. There remains only to enjoy your handiwork. For crochet done in pieces, however, the last step is to sew the pieces together (and perhaps to add an edging). Most crocheted accessories for the home such as afghans, tablecloths and bedspreads lie flat. They must be joined in a seam that will allow the pieces to lie side by side without ridges. Overcasting creates a flat seam and is a good method to use. Hold the pieces with wrong sides together and edges matching. Using a tapestry needle and matching thread, secure the thread at one corner and then take the needle through the individual stitches along the sides of the pieces. Where you are joining a top edge to a top edge (and in the case of pieces made in the round, this includes all the edges), the overcasting stitches will give a regular diagonal stitch when opened out. If you want to feature these stitches, use a contrasting color. This method of joining pieces is illustrated on page 153 under Finishing an afghan. See also Working an invisible seam on page 153.

Another method of joining pieces of crochet is to crochet them together. This makes a feature of the seam and is quicker than overcasting. Place the right sides of the pieces together with edges matching and work along the seam with slip stitches. Placing the wrong sides together and working the slip stitches on the right side forms a ridge which can make a very distinctive feature. For emphasis, raise the ridge by working in single crochet instead of slip stitch and perhaps use a contrasting color. See also Crochet seaming on page 154.

In traditional Irish crochet, pieces are linked together with short lengths of chain stitches. This method can also be used on other openwork for an invisible join.

Working in fine cotton

Fine cotton in a range of weights (see page 9) is used with steel hooks (see page 11) to make a wide range of delicate home accessories from lacy edgings to tablecloths.

When working with fine cotton, keep it taut by threading it between the fingers of the left hand; the crochet should be firm with no loose stitches. It should be difficult to insert the hook into the top of a stitch. Keep the working loops well down the neck or narrow part of the hook. After completing a stitch, tighten the top by pulling back the thread with the fingers of the left hand.

Beginning

In working a number of pieces in the round, be sure all the centers are the same size. Leave a tail of about six inches before the first slip knot. After completing the piece, thread the tail through a fine sewing needle and weave it through the stitches of the first round. Put a thin knitting needle through the center of the circle, pull up the tail tightly and secure. Slide out the knitting needle.

Work a foundation chain fairly loosely; otherwise the lower edge will pucker. If the foundation chain is too tight, undo it and start again. If it is too loose, run a thread through and tighten.

Joining thread

Cotton thread up to size 20 can usually be spliced (see page 148). Finer cottons should be joined in a piece of solid pattern. Thread the new end into a fine sewing needle and work through the old yarn for about four inches leaving loose ends of the same length. Leave surplus ends at the back of the work and darn in separately at the end.

Finishing

Work the last stitch of the final row very carefully, and after cutting the yarn, do not pull too tightly. Thread the yarn into a sewing needle and work through the tops of the adjacent stitches. Pressing should be avoided as it will flatten the work. Instead, dampen or wash the work, pin it to the correct size and shape with rustproof pins. Leave to dry. Starch any ruffled edges and support with wedges or tissue paper during drying.

Creating an original

For those crocheters who want to create their own designs, *Crochet For a Beautiful Home* provides alternative stitch patterns in a variety of yarns and colors with many projects and alternative ideas for using them.

A few ground rules in design may also help.

Color

One of the easiest and most effective ways to create an original is with color. Planning is essential; it makes the difference between a harmonious whole and a hodge-podge. When using elaborate shapes or several shapes in a project, it is best to use a simple color scheme — one or two colors or several shades of one color. When you want to use many or sharply contrasting colors, use simple shapes. Map your design on graph paper and color it in to get an idea of the overall effect. Make samples of all the colors in the stitch you plan to use to be sure they go together. Some colors that appear very bright on their own lose their impact when combined with others, and some gain in intensity from their neighbors.

Stitches and yarn

To get ideas for stitch patterns, look through all the Alternative sections in the book, not just the one with the pattern you intend to use. Buy a ball of the yarn you are considering and try stitch patterns. In general, use simple, smooth yarn for busy or heavily textured patterns. If you want to use several stitch patterns or yarns in one project, make swatches in all of them to make sure they will work to the same gauge. If not, you may have to change the yarn or stitch or use a different hook. Work out the design on graph paper and try the different swatches together. Use a simple overall pattern such as stripes or a checkerboard if you are using elaborate textures or yarns.

Motifs

Some of the patterns include a picture or design on a plain crochet fabric or mesh. You can alter these designs by substituting your own motif. To get ideas for motifs, look at pictures in magazines or books or use your own photographs. You can also use letters or create an abstract design.

Make a swatch of the background fabric with the yarn, hook and stitch you plan to use. Measure the number of stitches and rows in a four-inch square and then work out the number of stitches and rows you will need in order for the final item to be the size you want. Draw this shape on graph paper with one box representing each stitch or filet square. Decide where you want to place the motif and how big you want it to be. Draw or trace the motif you have selected and reduce or enlarge it as necessary (see below). Plot the motif on the graph.

Enlarging or reducing a design

Trace you motif or try a number of sketches until you get what you want and then enclose the motif in a square or rectangle. Draw another square or rectangle in the same proportions as the first in the size you want the motif to be. If the second square or rectangle is to be larger, align the first at the bottom left-hand corner of a larger piece of paper. Draw a diagonal line from the lower left-hand corner of the small shape through the upper right-hand corner and continue it to the edge of the larger sheet of paper. Now extend the line along the lower edge of the smaller shape to the right until it reaches the length you want the second shape to be. Draw a line at right angles to this line up to the diagonal line. This gives you two sides of the larger square. Draw the other two lines to complete it. To make the second shape smaller, place a smaller piece of paper on top of the first and reverse the process.

Draw a grid of equal size squares over the first square or rectangle. Cover the second shape with a grid containing the same number of squares as the first. Transfer the motif by drawing it square by square onto the second grid.

You can transfer the motif from the second shape to the graph paper by putting it behind the graph paper in the appropriate location, holding both up to a window and tracing it.

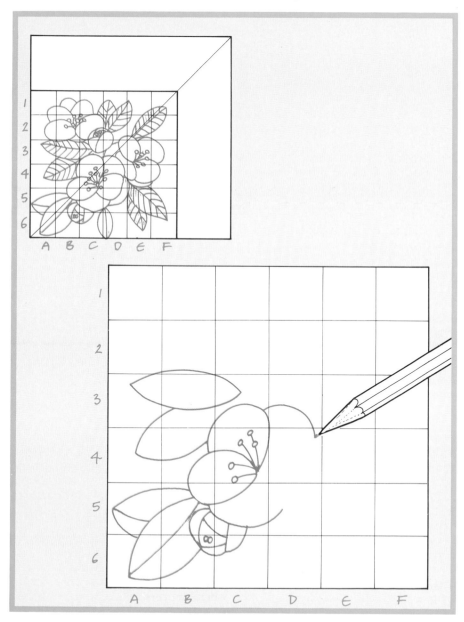

15

Patterns and alternatives

Among the 35 patterns on the following pages, you will find something for every room in the house. They range from straw mats and a child's sheep rug to place mats and afghans. And many patterns have alternative stitch patterns that can be substituted to vary the project as well as alternative ideas for using the stitch patterns and techniques.

Afghans

Pastel polygon afghan

Polygons are geometric shapes ranging from regular hexagons and octagons to flower-style medallions. Colorful polygons are usually worked in the round and sewn or crocheted together to make afghans and many other household accessories. This afghan, formed from hexagons in three different color combinations, is beautiful enough to become a treasured family heirloom.

Size

Afghan measures approx 53in × 70in

Gauge

Each motif measures 5in in diameter, measured between widest points
To save time, check your gauge.

Materials

Sport or double knitting yarn
16oz in main color, (A)
15oz each contrast colors, (B) and (C)
6oz each contrast colors, (D), (E) and (F)
4oz each contrast colors, (G), (H) and (J)
Size G crochet hook

Hexagon 1

Using size G hook and F, ch5, sl st into first ch to form a circle.
1st round Ch 3, leaving last loop of each st on hook work 2dc into circle, yo and draw through all 3 loops on hook — 2dc cluster formed — , (ch3, leaving last loop of each st on hook work 3dc into circle, yo and draw through all 4 loops on hook — 3dc cluster formed) 5 times, ch3, sl st to top of first 3ch. 6 3ch sps.
Break off F. Join in H.
2nd round Ch 2, 4hdc into first 3ch sp, 5hdc into each 3ch sp to end, sl st to top of first 2ch. 30 sts.
Break off H. Join in E.
3rd round Ch 3, skip first st, 1dc into next st, (2dc into next st, 1dc into each of next 4 sts) 5 times, 2dc into next st, 1dc into each of next 2 sts, sl st to top of first 3ch. 36 sts.
Break off E. Join in B.

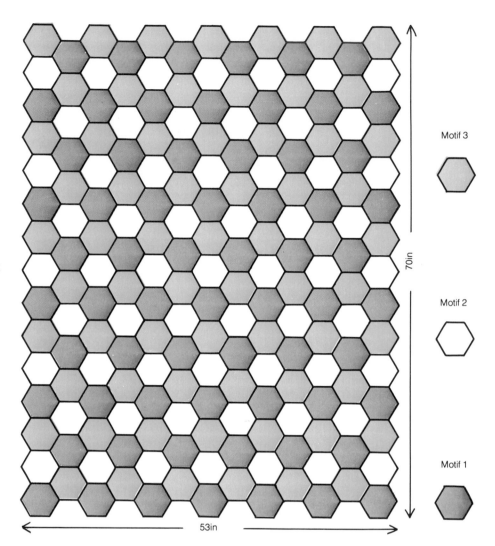

Motif 3

Motif 2

70in

Motif 1

53in

4th round Ch 1, 1sc into first st, (2sc into next st, 1sc into each of next 2sts) 11 times, 2sc into next st, 1sc into next st, sl st to first ch. 48 sts.

5th round Ch 1, 1sc into first st, (ch1, skip next st, 1hdc into next st, 2dc into each of next 2 sts, 1hdc into next st, ch1, skip next st, 1sc into each of next 2 sts) 6 times, ending last rep with 1sc, sl st to first ch.

6th round Ch 3, 3dc cluster into base of first 3ch, *ch 1, skip next sc and hdc, 1dc into next sp between hdc and dc, skip next 2dc, (4dc, ch2, 4dc) into next sp between 2 pairs of dc, skip next 2dc, 1dc into next sp between dc and hdc, ch1, skip next hdc and sc, leaving last loop of each st on hook work 4dc into next sp between next 2sc, yo and draw through all 5 loops on hook — 4dc cluster formed —, rep from * ending last rep with skip next hdc and sc, sl st to top of first 3dc cluster.
Fasten off.
Make 64 more hexagons in the same way.

Hexagon 2

Using size G hook and D, ch4, sl st into first ch to form a circle.

1st round Ch 1, 12sc into circle, sl st to first ch. 12 sts.
Break off D. Join in C.

2nd round Ch 5, skip first st, (1dc into next st, ch 2) 11 times, sl st to 3rd of first 5ch. 12 2ch sps.
Break off C. Join in A.

3rd round Ch 3, 3dc cluster into first 2ch sp, ch3, (4dc cluster into next 2ch sp, ch 3) 11 times, sl st to top of first 3dc cluster. 12 3ch sps.

Do not break off A. Join in J.
4th round Ch 1, *4sc into next 3ch sp, rep from * to end. 48 sts.
Break off J. Cont in A.
5th and 6th rounds As Hexagon 1.
Fasten off.
Make another 58 hexagons in the same way.

Hexagon 3

Using size G hook and G, ch5, sl st into first ch to form a circle. Work as for Hexagon 1, using colors as follows:
1st round In G.
2nd round In F.
3rd round In D.
4th round In A.
5th and 6th rounds In C.

Fasten off.
Make 64 more hexagons in the same way.

Note: There should be a total of 189 hexagons: 65 of hexagon 1, 59 of hexagon 2 and 65 of hexagon 3.

To finish

Do not press.
Join hexagons as shown in the diagram on this page using overcast stitch. See Finishing an afghan, page 153.

Edging

Using size G hook and A, work 2 rounds of sc into outer edge of afghan, working 1sc into each st, and 3sc into sts at angles of hexagons.

Alternatives

Any of the polygon shapes below could be used to make an original afghan for your home. Or use one to make a tablecloth or bedspread.

Before beginning to make the shapes, sort out and decide on the yarns you wish to use. Make sure that they are all of the same weight, and arrange them into color groups. For a bright, eye-catching effect, use a wide variety of contrasting colors. Use a smaller number of colors in a wide range of tones for a more subtle shaded look. When you have worked enough shapes, place them on to a clean sheet, right sides up and arrange them in an overall design. This will help you decide whether you will like the final appearance of the afghan. Make more shapes as necessary.

There is usually no need to press the shapes before sewing them together because these crochet pieces usually lie flat of their own accord. If you must press, use a dry cloth and a cool iron; a hot iron and damp cloth would flatten the texture.

Hexagons can be seamed on all sides. Polygons with more than six sides must be caught together wherever they touch each other, creating a pretty openwork effect.

If the spaces between the shapes are exceptionally large, you can fill them with small crochet shapes in matching colors.

Polygon Patterns

1 Leaded window
Ch 8.
Base row 1dc into 6th ch from hook, (ch1, skip next ch, 1dc into next ch) twice. Turn.
1st and 2nd rows Ch4, skip first dc and sp, (1dc into next dc, ch 1) twice, skip last sp, 1dc into last st. Turn.
1st round (RS) Ch1, *1sc into first st, (1sc into next sp, 1sc into next st) twice, 1sc into next sp, 3sc into next st, 2sc into side of same st, 1sc into side of next st, 2sc into side of next st, 2sc into first dc of row, rep from * once more, sl st to first ch. 32 sts.

2nd round Ch14, (skip next 3sc, 1sc into next sc, 1sc into each of last 5ch, ch 9, skip next 3sc, 1sc into next sc, 1sc into each of last 3ch, ch11) 3 times, skip next 3sc, 1sc into next sc, 1sc into each of last 5ch, ch6, 1sc into each of first 3ch of 14ch worked at beg of round, sl st to sl st of last round. Fasten off.

2 Cluster
Ch 8, sl st into first ch to form a circle.
1st round Ch 1, 12sc into circle, sl st to first ch.
2nd round Ch 3, 1dc into first st, *ch3, leaving last loop of each st on hook work 2dc into next sc, yo and draw through all 3 loops on hook — 2dc cluster formed —, rep from * 10 times more, ch3, sl st to top of first 3ch.
3rd round Sl st to center of first 3ch sp, 1sc into same place as sl st, *ch4, 1 sc into next 3ch sp, rep from * 10 times more, ch4, sl st to top of first sc.

4th round Ch 1, *(2sc, ch3, 2sc) into next 4ch loop, rep from * 11 times more, sl st to first ch.

5th round Sl st to first ch of first 3ch loop, ch3, (1dc, ch4, 2dc cluster) into first 3ch loop, *(2dc cluster, ch4, 2dc cluster) into next 3ch loop, rep from * 10 times more, sl st to top of first 3ch. Fasten off.

3 Rose picot
Wind yarn 3 times around index finger to form a circle.
1st round Ch 1, 24sc into circle, sl st to first ch. 24sts.
2nd round Ch 1, 1sc into back loop only of first sc, *ch3, 1sc into stem of next sc — picot formed —, 1sc into

back loop only of next sc, rep from * 10 times more, picot into last sc, sl st to first ch. 12 picots.
3rd round Ch 8 to count as first tr and 4ch, *1tr between next 2 picots, ch4, rep from * 10 times more, sl st to 4th of first 8ch. 12 4ch sps.
4th round Ch1, *6sc into 4ch loop, rep from * 11 times more, sl st into first chain.
Fasten off.

4 Petal polygon
Ch 9, sl st into first ch to form a circle.
1st round Ch3, 3dc into circle, *ch5, 4dc into circle, rep from * 4 times more, ch5, sl st to top of first 3ch.
2nd round Ch3, skip first st, 1dc into each of next 3dc, *ch3, 1sc into next 5ch loop, ch3, 1dc into each of next 4dc, rep from * 4 times more, ch3, 1sc into last 5ch loop, ch3, sl st to top of first 3ch.
3rd round Ch 3, work next 3 dc tog, *(ch5, 1sc into next 3ch loop) twice, ch5, work next 4dc tog, rep from * 4 times more, (5ch, 1sc into next 3ch loop) twice, ch5, sl st to top of first 3ch. Fasten off.

5 Rosette
Ch 6, sl st into first ch to form a circle.
1st round Ch 3 to count as first dc, 17dc into circle, sl st to top of first 3ch. 18sts.

2nd round Ch 3, skip first 3dc, *1sc into next dc, ch3, skip next 2dc, rep from * 4 times more, ending with 1sc into same place as first 3ch.
3rd round *Ch 2, (1dc, yo, insert hook into sp, yo, draw through first loop on hook, yo, draw through first 2 loops on hook, yo, draw through rem 2 loops on hook — half tr formed —, 1tr, 1 half tr, 1dc) into next 3ch sp, ch2, sl st into next sc, rep from * 5 times more.
4th round Sl st to first tr, *ch8, sl st into next tr, rep from * 5 times more ending with sl st into first of 8ch worked at beg of round.
5th round Ch 2 to count as first tr, 11hdc into first 8ch sp, * 12hdc into next 8ch sp, rep from * 4 times more, sl st to top of first 2ch. Fasten off.

6 Popcorn star
Ch 12, sl st into first chain to form a circle.
1st round Ch 1, 16sc into circle, sl st to first ch. 16sc.
2nd round Ch 3, 3dc into first sc, remove hook from loop, insert hook into top of first 3ch and into loop just left, yo and draw through 2 loops on hook — 3dc popcorn formed —, *ch5, sl st into 3rd ch from hook — picot formed —, ch2, skip next sc, 4dc into next sc, remove hook from loop, insert hook into top of first dc and into loop just left, yo and draw through 2 loops on hook — 4dc popcorn formed —, rep from * 6 times more, ch2, picot, ch2, sl st into top of first 3ch.
3rd round Ch 1, 1sc into top of 3dc popcorn, *ch12, 1sc into top of next 4dc popcorn, rep from * 6 times more, ch12, sl st into first ch.
Fasten off.

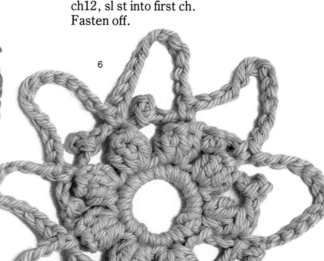

Striped afghan

Crochet stripes of red, orange, yellow, green, blue and violet for an authentic rainbow afghan.

Size
Approx 57in long by 33in wide

Gauge
15 sts and 9 rows to 4in over dc pat on size G crochet hook
To save time, check your gauge.

Materials
Knitting worsted or double knitting
6oz in main colors (A) and (B)
4oz each in contrast colors (C), (D), (E), (F) and (G)
Size G crochet hook

To make
Using size G hook and A ch 115.
Base row (RS) 1dc into 4th ch from hook, 1dc into each ch to end. Turn. 113 sts.
Pat row Ch 3, 1dc into each dc to end, working last dc into top of turning ch. Turn. 113 sts.
Cont to work as for pat row, working 2 rows of each color as follows: B, C, D, E, F and G.
These 14 rows form the pat. Rep them 8 times more. Fasten off.

Edging
1st round Using size G hook and with RS facing, join B to last dc worked, ch1, skip first dc, 1sc into top of each dc to turning ch, 3sc into top of turning ch to form corner, 3sc evenly into the row ends of each stripe, 3sc into first dc worked to form corner, 1sc into each ch to turning ch, 3sc into turning ch to form corner, 3sc evenly into row ends of each stripe to last dc worked in G, 3sc into last dc to form corner, join with a sl st to first ch.
2nd round Ch 1, *1sc into each sc to second of 3sc at corner, 3sc into corner sc *, rep from * to * 3 times more, 1sc into next sc, skip last sc, join to first ch with a sl st.
3rd round Ch 1, *1sc into each sc to second of 3sc at corner, 3sc into corner sc*, rep from * to * 3 times more, 1sc into each of next 2sc, skip last sc, join with a sl st to first ch.
4th-6th rounds Using A, continue to work in this way, working 3sc into each corner and skipping the last st on each round. Fasten off.

Striped patterns

1 Alternating stripes

Combine plain yarn with bouclé for texture and color.

Use 5 colors, A, B, C, D and E, and a bouclé yarn, F.

1st row Using A, work in dc.

2nd row and every other row (RS) Using F, work in sc.

3rd row Using B, as 1st row.

5th row Using C, as 1st row.

7th row Using D, as 1st row.

9th row Using E, as 1st row.

10th row Using F, as 2nd row.

1st–10th rows form pat. Rep them throughout.

2 Triple crochet stripes

Combine wide stripes of one color with narrow many-colored stripes.

Use 4 colors, A, B, C and D.

1st and every other row (RS) Using A, work in tr.

2nd row Using B, work in sc.

4th row Using C, work in hdc.

6th row Using D, as 2nd row.

1st–6th rows form pat. Rep them throughout.

To finish

Darn in all the ends neatly on the wrong side.

Do not press.

Alternatives

Choose your favorite colors and work a different version of the sparkling striped afghan. Or work a striped cover for a pillow.

Striped patterns are great fun to crochet and the work always seems to grow quickly. Choose another stitch pattern and a range of pastels or neutrals for a different effect. If you use different yarns together, be sure they are all of the same weight and work to the same gauge.

Aran afghan

The enduring appeal of Aran patterns — worked here in crochet — will make this afghan a family favorite. Four different stitches are used to make the squares, and the completed squares are then joined together.

Size

Approx 56in × 75in

Note: This afghan is made up of 48 squares (each approximately 9in square) in four different patterns. For easy reference we have given each pattern a letter — squares A, B, C and D.

Gauge

A, 4 pat repeats to 2in in width worked on size K hook

B, 3 pat repeats to 2in in width worked on size K hook

C, 8sc to 2in in width worked on size I hook

D, 2 pat repeats to 2in in width worked on size I hook

To save time, check your gauge.

Materials

100oz of Fisherman or knitting worsted yarn

Size I and size K crochet hooks

Square A (worked in even seed stitch)

Using size K hook, ch31 fairly loosely.

Base row (RS) Sl st into 3rd ch from hook, * 1hdc into next ch, sl st into next ch, rep from * to end. Turn.

Pat row Ch 2 to count as first hdc, skip first sl st, *sl st into next hdc, 1hdc into next sl st, rep from * to within turning ch, sl st into 2nd of first 2ch. Turn.

Rep the pat row until work measures 9in from beg. Fasten off.

Make 11 more squares in the same way.

Square B (worked in uneven berry stitch)

Using size K hook, ch30 fairly loosely.

Base row (RS) 1sc into 3rd ch from hook, then work 1sc into each ch to end. Turn.

1st row Ch 1, skip first sc, *yo, insert hook into next sc, yo and draw a loop through loosely, yo and draw through one loop on hook (3 loops on hook), yo, insert hook into same sc, yo and draw a loop through loosely (5 loops on hook), yo and draw through 4 loops on hook, yo and draw through rem 2 loops on hook — called B1 —, sl st into next sc, rep from * to last 2 sts, B1 into next sc, 1sc into 2nd of first 2ch. Turn.

2nd row Ch1, skip first sc, *sl st into next B1, 1sc into next sl st, rep from * to within last 2 sts, sl st into next B1, 1 sc into first ch. Turn.

3rd row Ch 1, skip first sc, *sl st into next sl st, B1 into next sc, rep from * to within last 2 sts, sl st into next sl st, 1sc into first ch. Turn.

4th row Ch 1, skip first sc, *1sc into next sl st, sl st into next B1, rep from * to within last 2 sts, 1 sc into next sl st, 1sc into first ch. Turn.

5th row Ch 1, skip first sc, *B1 into next sc, sl st into next sl st, rep from * to within last 2 sts, B1 into next sc, 1sc into first ch. Turn.

The 2nd to 5th rows form the pat. Cont in pat until work measures 9in from beg, ending with 2nd or 4th row. Fasten off.

Make 11 more squares in the same way.

Square C (worked in rib)

Using size I hook, ch32 fairly loosely.

Base row (WS) 1sc into 3rd ch from hook, 1sc into each ch to end. Turn.

Pat row Ch 1 to count as first sc, skip first sc, 1sc into each sc to end, placing the hook into the horizontal loop under the normal ch loop of the sc, 1sc into turning ch, turn.

Rep the pat row until work measures 9in from beg. Fasten off.

Make 11 more squares in the same way.

Square D (worked in lattice stitch)

Using size I hook, ch28 fairly loosely.

Base row (WS) 1dc into 3rd ch from hook, 1dc into each ch to end, turn.

1st row Working pat on front of the fabric work (yo) twice, insert hook into base of 3rd dc on base row from right to left, yo and draw a loop through, (yo and draw through 2 loops on hook) twice — called 1 open tr —, insert hook into top of first dc, yo and draw a loop through, yo and draw through all 3 loops on hook — called close 1tr —, 1sc in each of next 2dc, *1 open tr into base of same dc as before, skip next 2dc, 1 open tr in base of next dc, insert hook into top of dc after last sc worked, yo and draw a loop through, yo and draw through all 4 loops on hook — called close 2tr —, 1sc into each of next 2dc, rep from * to within last dc, 1 open tr into base of same dc as before, close 1 tr in last dc. Turn.

2nd row Ch 2 for first dc, skip first sc, 1dc into each sc to end. Turn. 28dc.

3rd row Ch 1 for first sc, skip first dc, 1sc into next dc, inserting hook from right to left under first tr 2 rows below, work 1 open tr, then work 1 open tr under next gr of 2tr, close 2tr, 1 sc in each of next 2dc, *1 open tr under same gr of 2tr as before, 1 open tr under next gr of 2tr, close 2tr, 1sc into each of next 2dc, rep from * to within last 2dc, 1 open tr, under same gr of 2tr as before, 1 open tr under last tr, close 2tr, 1sc into last dc. Turn.

4th row As 2nd pat row.

5th row 1 open tr under first gr of 2tr, close 1tr working into first dc, 1sc into

25

Patterns and alternatives

each of next 2dc, * 1 open tr under same gr of 2tr as before, 1 open tr under next gr of 2tr, close 2tr, 1sc into each of next 2dc, rep from * to within last dc, 1 open tr under same gr of 2tr as before, 1 open tr into last dc, close 2tr. Turn.

The 2nd to 5th rows form the pat. Cont to rep these rows until work measures 9in from beg, ending with a 5th row. Fasten off.

Make 11 more squares in the same way.

To finish

Overcast the squares tog on the WS of the work, following the diagram.

Border

With RS facing and using size K hook, join yarn to one corner and ch1 to count as first sc, work an uneven number of sc evenly along each edge with 3sc into the first 3 corners and 2sc into last corner, join with sl st to first ch. Turn. Work in uneven seed stitch as foll:

1st round Sl st into center sc at first corner, ch1 to count as first sc, * (sl st into next sc, 1hdc into next sc) to center sc at next corner, 3sc into center sc, rep from * all around edge ending with a sl st into first sl st, 2sc into same sc as sl st, sl st into first ch to complete the round. Turn.

2nd round Sl st into center sc at first corner, ch1 for first sc, * (1 hdc into next sc, sl st into sl st, 1hdc into next hdc, sl st into next sl st), to 3sc at next corner, 1hdc into next sc, 3sc into next sc, rep from * all around edge ending last rep with 1hdc into first sl st, 2sc into same sc as sl st, sl st into first ch to complete the round. Turn.

3rd round Sl st into center sc at first corner, ch1, * (1hdc into next sc, sl st into next hdc, 1hdc into next sl st, sl st into next hdc) to 3sc at next corner, 1hdc into next sc, 3sc into next sc, rep from * all around edge ending last rep with 1hdc into first sl st, 2sc into same sc as sl st, sl st into first ch to complete the round. Turn.

4th round Sl st into center sc at first corner, ch1, * (sl st into next sc, 1hdc into next hdc, sl st into next sl st, 1hdc into next hdc) to 3sc at next corner, sl st into next sc, 3sc into next sc, rep

C	B	A	D	C	B	A	D
D	C	B	A	D	C	B	A
A	D	C	B	A	D	C	B
B	A	D	C	B	A	D	C
C	B	A	D	C	B	A	D
D	C	B	A	D	C	B	A

56in

75in

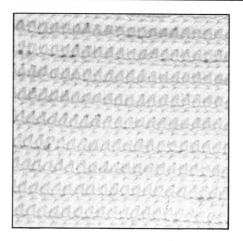

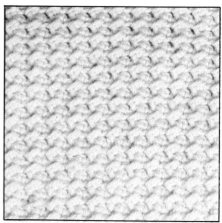

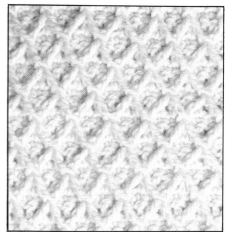

from * all around edge ending last rep with sl st into first sl st, 2sc into same sc as sl st, sl st into first ch to complete the round. Turn.

5th round Sl st into center sc at first corner, ch 1, * (sl st into next sc, 1hdc into next sl st, sl st into next hdc, 1hdc into next sl st) to 3sc at next corner, sl st into next sc, 3sc into next sc, rep from * all around edge, ending last rep with sl st into first sl st, 2sc into same sc as sl st, sl st to first ch to complete the round. Turn.

Rep the 2nd, 3rd and 4th rounds once more. Fasten off.

Ruffled baby afghan

**This technique for making ruffles creates a wonderfully
thick fabric, ideal for keeping baby snug.**

Size
27½in × 15¾in

Gauge
6tr and 3 rows to 3⅜in over mesh
when ruffles have been worked

To save time, check your gauge.

Materials
3oz sport yarn in main color (A)
6oz in contrast colors (B) and (C)
5oz in contrast color (D)

Size F crochet hook

Note: See Working around the stem on
page 149.

Patterns and alternatives

Mesh backing

With A and size F hook, ch99.
1st row 1tr into 7th ch from hook, * ch1, skip next ch, 1tr into next ch, rep from * to end, turn.
2nd row Ch 5, *1tr into next tr, ch1, rep from * to last tr, 1tr into 2nd ch of turning ch, turn.
Rep 2nd row 11 times. Fasten off.

Ruffles

Turn work sideways and work across the mesh rows.
1st row With B and size F hook, join with sl st to stem of 1st tr, ch4, 13tr around stem of same tr, *work 14tr around stem of next tr, rep from * to end. Fasten off.
This row forms the pat. Cont in this way throughout the mesh in the foll color sequence: 3 more rows in B, * 2 in C, 2 in D, 2 in C, 2 in B, 2 in D, 2 in C, 2 in D, 2 in B, rep from * until 10 rows remain. Work 8 more rows in pat, then work 2 more rows in B. 46 rows.

Edging

With RS of work facing, join A with sl st to corner of mesh. Work sc all around edge of mesh as foll:
1st row 4sc into each sp at ends, 2sc into each sp up sides, with (1sc, ch1, 1sc) into each corner sp. Join to 1st sc with sl st. Turn.
2nd row *Ch 1, 1sc into each sc to corner, (1sc, ch1, 1sc) into 1ch sp, rep from * to end, join with sl st to 1st ch. Turn. Rep 2nd row 3 times more. Fasten off. Darn in all ends.

To finish

Do not press.

Special technique — triple crochet ruffles

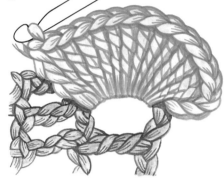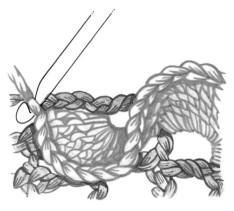

1 *These ruffles are worked on a background one-triple crochet, one-chain mesh. Turn the mesh sideways so that the foundation chain now forms the right-hand edge and triple crochet stitches lie horizontally. Rejoin the yarn to the stem of the second triple as shown.*

2 *Make four chains to count as the first triple. Work about 12 triples around the stem of the first stitch — the number can be varied as required.*

3 *Pushing the stitches together, work 13 triples around the stem of each mesh triple to the LH (i.e. top) edge. Fasten off.*

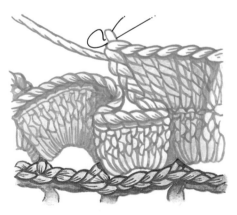

4 *Return to the right-hand (i.e. lower) edge of the work and rejoin the yarn to the next triple crochet. Work another row of ruffles as before. Work ruffles along every line of mesh triples, omitting the last line of triples.*

5 *Longer ruffles can be formed by turning and working a second row of triples into the ruffles. Working double crochet around the triple stitches forms shorter ruffles. Rows of single crochet can be worked into the ruffles.*

Alternatives

Use different yarns, color, and stitches to create a variety of ruffles.

Any of the alternative ruffles could be used to vary the baby blanket or to make a larger blanket or a pillow cover. Before you work the ruffles, experiment on a small swatch of base mesh to make sure that the ruffles will hang well.

Remember that a great deal of yarn is needed for ruffles, so buy extra when substituting patterns or adding extra ruffles.

Ruffle patterns

1 Simple double crochet ruffles

Even simple double crochet ruffles, worked in one color on a one-double crochet, two-chain mesh, can form a very attractive textured fabric.

2 Glitter-striped ruffles

Use a plain and a glitter yarn. Using the plain yarn, work double crochet ruffles on a one-double, two-chain mesh, working 13 doubles around each stitch and into intervening two-chain spaces.
2nd row Using glitter yarn, work in sc.
3rd row Using plain yarn, work in dc.
4th row As 2nd row.
Fasten off.

3 Long ruffles

Use a mohair yarn to work triple crochet ruffles on a one-triple crochet, one-chain mesh. Make each ruffle from two rows of triple crochet and use a different color for each separate ruffle.

4 Multi-colored ruffles

Use five colors, A, B, C, D and E. Using A, work double crochet ruffles on a one-triple crochet, one-chain mesh. Work 14 triples around the stem of each triple. Work rows of single crochet using each of the remaining four colors.
Fasten off.

Flower garden afghan

While away long winter evenings making flowers for a vivid garden afghan.

Size

Approx 69in long by 54in wide

Gauge

One hexagon measures 3½in across the widest part worked on size F crochet hook
To save time, check your gauge.

Materials

23oz of sports or double knitting yarn in main color (A)
4oz in each of contrast colors, (B) and (C)
3oz in each of contrast colors, (D), (E), (F), (G) and (H)
Size F crochet hook

Hexagon

Using size F hook and A, ch6, sl st into first ch to form a ring.
1st round Ch 6, 1tr into ring, *ch2, 1tr into ring, rep from * 9 times more, ch2, sl st into 4th of the 6ch.
2nd round Sl st into next sp, ch3, 1dc, 2ch and 2dc into same sp as sl st, *3dc into next sp, 2dc, 2ch and 2dc all into next sp, rep from * 4 times more, 3dc into next sp, sl st into top of ch3.
Fasten off.
Make 248 more motifs in A, then make 36 each in B and C, 32 in D and 30 each in E, F, G and H.

To finish

Darn in all loose ends on each hexagon. Following the diagram for position, overcast hexagons together. See Finishing an afghan, page 153.
Using A, work a row of sc around outer edge, working 2sc into each sp at outer corners of each motif and working 2sc tog at inner corners (i.e. at each join).

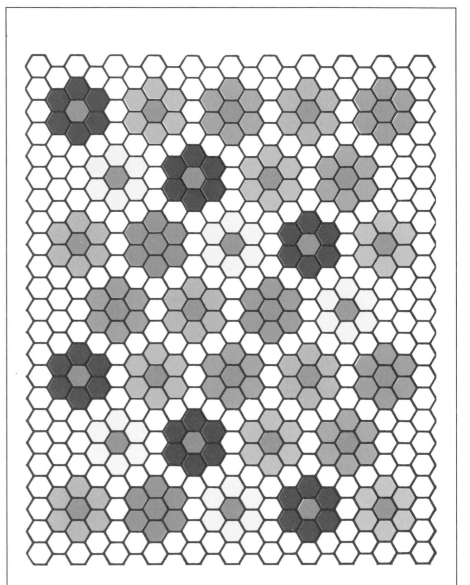

Diagram showing the color plan of each flower garden bordered by a white meandering path.

Scatter pillows

Chevron pillows

Make lots of comfortable pillows — all in distinctive designs but united by a common color scheme and an attractive chevron pattern.

Size

Each pillow measures about 16in square

Gauge

18 sts and 9 rows to 4in over plain dc worked on size E hook
To save time, check your gauge.

Materials

Sport yarn
1st pillow 4oz in main color (A)
2oz in contrast color (B)
2nd pillow 2oz each in (A), (B), (C) and (D)
3rd pillow As given for 2nd pillow
4th pillow 4oz in main color (A)

2oz each in (B), (C) and (D)
Size E crochet hook
16in square pillow forms

Note: See Working chevrons on page 155.

From left, first, second, third, fourth pillows

Patterns and alternatives

First pillow

Using size E hook and A, ch77.
1st row 1dc into 4th ch from hook, 1dc into each of next 22ch, skip 2ch, 1dc into each of next 24ch, 3dc into next ch, 1dc into each of next 24ch. 75 sts.
2nd row Sl st into 2nd dc, ch3, 1dc into each of next 23dc, 3dc into next dc, 1dc into each of next 24dc, skip 2dc, 1dc into each of next 22dc, 2dc into 3rd of 3ch.
3rd row Ch 3, 1dc into same place (edge st), 1dc into each of next 22dc, skip 2dc, 1dc into each of next 24dc, 3dc into next dc, 1dc into each of next 24dc, turn.
The 2nd and 3rd rows form pat.
Continue in pat, working 11 rows more in A, 6 rows in B, 32 rows in A, 6 rows in B, 12 rows in A.
Fasten off.

Second pillow

Using size E hook and C, ch78.
1st row 1dc into 4th ch from hook, 1dc into each of next 3ch, *3dc into next ch, 1dc into each of next 5ch, skip 2ch, 1dc into each of next 5ch, rep from * 4 times more, 3dc into next ch, 1dc into each of next 5ch. 78 sts.
2nd row Sl st into 2nd dc, ch3, 1dc into each of next 4dc, *3dc into next dc, 1dc into each of next 5dc, skip 2dc, 1dc into each of next 5dc, rep from * 4 times more, 3dc into next dc, 1dc into each of next 5dc, turn.
The 2nd row forms pat.
Continue in pat, working 2 rows more in C, (2 rows in A, 4 rows in B, 2 rows in A, 4 rows in D, 2 rows in A, 4 rows in C) 3 times, 2 rows in A, 4 rows in B, 2 rows in A, 4 rows in D, 2 rows in A.
Fasten off.

Third pillow

Using size E hook and B, ch68.
1st row 1dc into 4th ch from hook, 1dc into each of next 5ch, *3dc into next ch, 1dc into each of next 7ch, skip 2ch, 1dc into each of next 7ch, rep from * twice more, 3dc into next ch, 1dc into each of next 7ch. 68 sts.
2nd row Sl st into 2nd dc, ch3, 1dc into each of next 6dc, *3dc into next dc, 1dc into each of next 7dc, skip 2dc, 1dc into each of next 7dc, rep from * twice more, 3dc into next dc, 1dc into each of next 7dc, turn.
The 2nd row forms pat.
Continue in pat, working 6 rows more in B, 3 rows in C, 5 rows in A, 3 rows in D, 32 rows in B, 3 rows in D, 5 rows in A, 3 rows in C, 8 rows in B.
Fasten off.

Fourth pillow

Using size E hook and A, ch71.
1st row 1dc into 4th ch from hook, 1dc into each of next 6ch, * skip 2ch, 1dc into each of next 7ch, 3dc into next ch, 1dc into each of next 7ch, rep from * twice more, skip 2ch, 1dc into each of next 8ch. 67 sts.
2nd row Ch 3, 1dc into same place (edge st), 1dc into each of next 7dc, *skip 2dc, 1dc into each of next 7dc, 3dc into next dc, 1dc into each of next 7dc, rep from * twice more, skip 2dc, 1dc into each of next 7dc, 2dc into next dc. 69 sts.
The 2nd row forms pat.
Continue in pat, working (2 rows in C, 4 rows in A, 2 rows in D, 4 rows in A, 2 rows in B, 4 rows in A) twice, 2 rows in B, 4 rows in A, 2 rows in D, 4 rows in A, 2 rows in C, 4 rows in A, 2 rows in B, 4 rows in A, 2 rows in D, 4 rows in A, 2 rows in C, 2 rows in A.
Fasten off.

To finish

Do not press.
For all pillows, fold work in half and join the two sides with an invisible seam. (See Working an invisible seam on page 153.) Insert pillow form and join the remaining seam.

Alternatives

Create dazzling zigzag afghans as well as pillow covers using simple and fancy chevron patterns.

Simple chevron patterns can be varied easily by working the stitches in a slightly different way. For example, a double crochet chevron looks very different when the double crochet stitches are worked into the backs of the stitches below or when one-chain spaces are substituted for doubles. More complicated chevron patterns are difficult to alter because they have varying gauges and, in many cases, large stitch multiples. If you do decide to use a fancy chevron, check your gauge very carefully indeed.
Fancy — and to a lesser extent, simple — chevrons may cause difficulties when counting stitches because of the increased and decreased stitches. Always count every stitch of an increased group; count each decreased group as one stitch.
The finished result will look more professional if you pay special attention to finishing. If the yarn allows, press the work carefully. Use an invisible seam. It will help you match striped patterns exactly. See Working an invisible seam on page 153.
Fancy chevrons look best worked in a plain yarn to show off the lacy or textured fabric. Simple chevrons can be made in fancy yarns, but plan the work in such a way that the zigzag pattern is not hidden by the hairs or loops of the yarn.

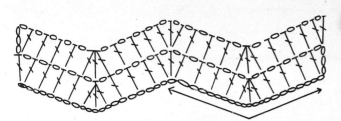

1 Mesh chevron

Use 2 colors, A and B. Using A, make a multiple of 20ch plus 5 extra. Rep pat row throughout — work is reversible. Work base and pat row in A, then cont in stripe sequence of 2 rows B, 2 rows A.

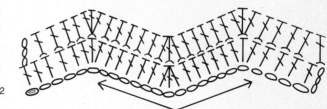

2 Overlapping chevron

Use 2 colors, A and B. Using A, make a multiple of 14ch plus 13 extra. Rep pat row throughout. Work base and pat row in A, then cont in strip sequence of 2 rows B, 2 rows A.

Chevron patterns

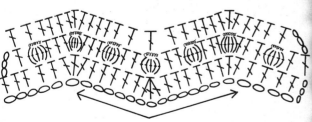

3 Cluster chevron

Use 2 colors, A and B. Using A, make a multiple of 14ch plus 13 extra. 1st (RS) and 2nd rows form pat. Work first 4 rows in A, then cont in stripe sequence of 3 rows B, 3 rows A.

Geometric pillows

Relax against these comfortable pillows crocheted in hard-wearing yarn. Make them in colors to match your home.

Sizes

Striped pillow measures approx 18in between widest points
Bobble pillow measures approx 18in between widest points
Lacy pillow measures approx 18in between widest points

Gauge

Striped pillow 17 sts and 10 rows to 4in over hdc pat
Bobble pillow 18 sts and 10 rows to 4in over hdc
Lacy pillow 16 sts and 8 rows to 4in over dc
To save time, check your gauge.

Materials

Knitting worsted or double knitting yarn
Striped pillow 2oz of main color, (A) 2oz of contrast color, (B)
Bobble pillow 3oz
Lacy pillow 2oz
Size F crochet hook
½yd of satin or other material to cover each pillow
Stuffing

Striped pillow

Using size F hook and A, ch4, sl st into first ch to form a circle.
1st round Using A, ch1, 11sc into circle, sl st to first ch. 12 sts.

2nd round Ch 2 to count as first hdc, * 3hdc into next sc, 1 hdc into next sc, rep from * 4 times more, 3hdc into next sc, sl st to top of first 2ch. 24 sts.
3rd round Using B, ch2 to count as first hdc, 1hdc into next hdc, *3hdc into next hdc, 1hdc into each of next 3hdc, rep from * 4 times more, 3hdc into next hdc, 1hdc into next hdc, sl st to top of first 2ch. 36 sts.
4th round Using A, ch2 to count as first hdc, 1hdc into each of next 2hdc, * 3hdc into next hdc, 1hdc into each of next 5hdc, rep from * 4 times more, 3hdc into next hdc, 1hdc into each of next 2hdc, sl st to top of first 2ch. 48 sts.
Work 16 more rounds in this way, inc 12 hdc on each round as set and working in stripe sequence as follows: A, B, B, A, B, A, B, A, A, B, A, B, B, A, A, B. 240hdc. Fasten off.

Note: The above stripe sequence can be varied as desired.

Bobble pillow

Using size F hook, ch4, sl st into first ch to form a circle.
1st and 2nd rounds As Striped pillow.
3rd round Ch 2 to count as first st, (yo, insert hook into next st and draw through a loop) 3 times, yo and draw through first 6 loops on hook, yo and draw through rem 2 loops on hook — bobble formed — *3hdc into next st, bobble into next st, 1hdc into next st, bobble into next st, rep from * 4 times more, 3hdc into next st, bobble into next st, sl st to top of first 2ch. 12 bobbles.
4th round Ch 2 to count as first st, bobble into next st, 1hdc into next st, *3hdc into next st, (1hdc into next st, bobble into next st) twice, 1hdc into next st, rep from * 4 times more, 3hdc into next st, 1hdc into next st, bobble into next st, sl st to top of first 2ch.
5th round Ch 2 to count as first st, bobble into next st, 1hdc into next st, bobble into next st, *3hdc into next st, (bobble into next st, 1hdc into next st) 3 times, bobble into next st, rep from * 4 times more, 3hdc into next st, bobble into next st, 1hdc into next st, bobble in next st, sl st to top of first 2ch. 24 bobbles.
6th round Ch 2 to count as first st, (bobble into next st, 1hdc into next st) twice, *3hdc into next st, (1hdc into next st, bobble into next st) 4 times, 1hdc into next st, rep from * 4 times more, 3hdc into next st, (1hdc into next st, bobble into next st) twice, sl st to top of first 2ch.
7th round Ch 2 to count as first st, (bobble into next st, 1hdc into next st) twice, bobble into next st, *3hdc into next st, (bobble into next st, 1hdc into next st) 5 times, bobble into next st, rep from * 4 times more, 3hdc into next st, (bobble into next st, 1hdc into next st) twice, bobble into next st, sl st to top of first 2ch. 36 bobbles.
8th round Ch 2 to count as first st, (bobble into next st, 1hdc into next st) 3 times, *3hdc into next st, (1hdc into next st, bobble into next st) 6 times, 1hdc into next st, rep from * 4 times more, 3hdc into next st, (1hdc into next st, bobble into next st) 3 times, sl st to top of first 2ch.
9th round Ch 2 to count as first st, (bobble into next st, 1hdc into next st) 3 times, 1hdc into next st, *3hdc into next st, (bobble into next st, 1hdc into next st) 7 times, 1hdc into next st, rep from * 4 times, 3hdc into next st, (bobble into next st, 1hdc into next st) 3 times, bobble into next st, sl st to top of first 2ch. 42 bobbles.

Special technique — working geometric shapes

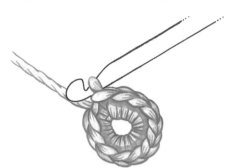

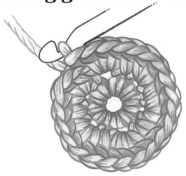

1 *To work any geometric shape you increase at each corner, thus adding extra stitches on each edge on every round. For a clear example of this technique, see the directions for the hexagonal striped pillow on page 36. After the first round of 12 stitches, begin to work corners on second round.*

2 *During the second round, 12 stitches and six corners are added. Each corner is formed from three half doubles worked into one stitch, with one half double on each edge. There should be 24 stitches in all including the two chains worked at the beginning of each round to form the first stitch.*

3 *On every following round, work 3 half doubles into the center half double at each corner to keep the corners correct and to increase 12 stitches on each round. An octagonal motif is worked in much the same way, except that 8, rather than 6, corners must be formed.*

10th round Ch 2 to count as first st, (bobble into next st, 1hdc into next st) twice, 1hdc into each of next 4 sts, *3hdc into next st, (1hdc into next st, bobble into next st) 6 times, 1hdc into each of next 5 sts, rep from * 4 times more, 3hdc into next st, (1hdc into next st, bobble into next st) 4 times, sl st to top of first 2ch. 36 bobbles.

11th round Ch 2 to count as first st, bobble into next st, 1hdc into each of next 8 sts, *3hdc into next st, (bobble into next st, 1hdc into next st) 6 times, 1hdc into each of next 7 sts, rep from * 4 times more, 3hdc into next st, (bobble into next st, 1hdc into next st) 4 times, bobble into next st, sl st to top of first 2ch.

12th round Ch 2 to count as first st, 1hdc into each of next 10sts, *3hdc into next st, (1hdc into next st, bobble into next st) 5 times, 1hdc into next 11 sts, rep from * 4 times more, 3hdc into next st, (1hdc into next st, bobble into next st) 5 times, sl st to top of first 2ch. 30 bobbles.

13th round Ch 2 to count as first st, 1hdc into each of next 11 sts, *3hdc into next st, (bobble into next st, 1hdc into next st) 5 times, 1hdc into each of next 13 sts, rep from * 4 times more, 3hdc into next st, (bobble into next st,

1hdc into next st) 5 times, 1hdc into next st, sl st to top of first 2ch.

14th round Ch 2 to count as first st, 1hdc into each of next 12 sts, *3hdc into next st, (1hdc into next st, bobble into next st) 4 times, 1hdc into each of next 17 sts, rep from * 4 times more, 3hdc into next st, (1hdc into next st, bobble into next st) 4 times, 1hdc into each of next 4hdc, sl st to top of first 2ch. 24 bobbles.

15th round Ch 2 to count as first st, 1hdc into each of next 13 sts, *3hdc into next st, (bobble into next st, 1hdc into next st) 4 times, 1hdc into each of next 19sts, rep from * 4 times more, 3hdc into next st, (bobble into next st, 1hdc into next st) 4 times, 1hdc into each of next 5 sts, sl st to top of first 2ch.

16th round Ch 2 to count as first st, 1hdc into each of next 14 sts, *3hdc into next st, (1hdc into next st, bobble into next st) 3 times, 1hdc into each of next 23 sts, rep from * 4 times more, 3hdc into next st, (1hdc into next st, bobble into next st) 3 times, 1hdc into each of next 8 sts, sl st to top of first 2ch. 18 bobbles.

17th round Ch 2 to count as first st, 1hdc into each of next 15 sts, *3hdc into next st, (bobble into next st, 1hdc

into next st) 3 times, 1hdc into each of next 25 sts, rep from * 4 times more, 3hdc into next st, (bobble into next st, 1hdc into next st) 3 times, 1hdc into each of next 9 sts, sl st to to top of first 2ch.

18th round Ch 2 to count as first st, 1hdc into each of next 16 sts, *3hdc into next st, (1hdc into next st, bobble into next st) twice, 1hdc into each of next 29 sts, rep from * 4 times more, 3hdc into next st, (1hdc into next st, bobble into next st) twice, 1hdc into each of next 12 sts, sl st to top of first 2ch, 12 bobbles.

19th round Ch 2 to count as first st, 1hdc into each of next 17 sts, *3hdc into next st, (bobble into next st, 1hdc into next st) twice, 1hdc into each of next 31 sts, rep from * 4 times more, 3hdc into next st, (bobble into next st, 1hdc into next st) twice, 1hdc into each of next 13 sts, sl st to top of first 2ch.

20th round Ch 2 to count as first st, 1hdc into each of next 18 sts, *3hdc into next st, 1hdc into next st, bobble into next st, 1hdc into each of next 35 sts, rep from * 4 times more, 3hdc into next st, 1hdc into next st, bobble into next st, 1hdc into each of next 16 sts, sl st to top of 2nd ch. 6 bobbles.
Fasten off.

Lacy pillow

Using size F hook, ch4.

1st round 11dc into 4th ch from hook, sl st to 4th of first 4ch. 12 sts.

2nd round Ch 1 to count as first sc, 1 sc into same place as sl st, 2sc into each st to end, sl st to first ch. 24 sts.

3rd round 1sc into same place as sl st, *ch3, skip next sc, 1sc into next sc, rep from *, ending with 3ch, sl st to first sc. 12 loops.

4th round Sl st to next loop, ch3, 9dc into same loop, *10dc into next loop, rep from *, ending with sl st to 3rd of first 3ch.
Fasten off.

5th round With RS facing and working behind previous 2 rounds, join yarn to any free sc on 2nd round, 1sc into same place as join, *ch4, 1sc into next free sc, rep from *, ending with 4ch, sl st to first sc. 12 loops.

6th round Sl st to center of first 4ch loop, 1sc into same loop, *ch5, 1sc into next 4ch loop, rep from *, ending with 2ch, 1dc into first sc.

7th round 1sc into loop just formed, *ch16, sl st into 13th ch from hook, ch3, 1sc into next loop, rep from *, omitting 1sc at end of last rep, sl st to first sc.

8th round Ch 4, *17dc into next 13ch loop — petal formed —, ch1, 1dc into next sc, ch1, rep from *, omitting 1dc and 1ch at end of last rep, sl st to 3rd of first 4ch. 12 petals.
Fasten off.

9th round With RS facing, skip first 8dc of any petal and rejoin yarn to next st, 1sc into same place as join, *ch9, skp first 8dc on next petal, (1hdc, ch3, 1hdc) into next st, ch9, skip first 8dc on next petal, 1sc into next dc, rep from * to end, omitting 1sc at end of last rep, sl st to first sc.

10th round Ch 3 to count as first dc, *9dc into next 9ch loop, 1dc into next hdc, 5dc into next 3ch loop, 1dc into next hdc, 9dc into next 9ch loop, 1dc into next sc, rep from *, omitting 1dc at end of last rep, sl st to 3rd of first 3ch. 156dc.

11th round Ch 3 to count as first dc, 1dc into each of next 12dc, *3dc into next dc, 1dc into each of next 25dc, rep from *, omitting 13dc at end of last rep, sl st to 3rd of first 3ch. 168dc.

12th round Ch 3 to count as first dc, 1dc into each of next 13dc, *3dc into next dc, 1dc into each of next 27dc, rep from *, omitting 14dc at end of last rep, sl st to third of first 3ch. 180dc.

13th and 14th rounds Cont to inc 12dc on each round as set. 204dc.
Fasten off.

To finish

For all three pillows:
Using the crochet as a guide and adding a ⅝in seam allowance, cut out 2 pieces of material for the cover. With right sides together, stitch them together, leaving an opening for stuffing. Turn, stuff and sew up opening. Using matching thread, slip stitch crochet to one side of pillow.

Alternatives

Use large hexagons or octagons in different stitch and color patterns to make useful — and beautiful — pillows for your home.

Most hexagons and octagons can be enlarged to make covers for pillows of any size. To work out how to increase, count the number of stitches added on each of the early rounds and continue in the same way.
In most alternative patterns, the sequence of increasing is given so you will not have to work it out. If you prefer to work lots of small hexagons, you can join them to form pillow covers or afghans. Small octagons leave gaps when joined, but these can be filled with pieces of plain crochet.

Geometric motif patterns

1 Ribbed hexagon

Ch 4, sl st to first ch to form a circle.

1st round Ch 3 to count as first dc, (1dc, ch1, 1dc) 5 times into circle, 1dc into circle, ch1, sl st to 3rd of first 3ch. 12dc.

1

2nd round Sl st into first dc and first ch sp, ch4 to count as first dc and 1ch sp, 1dc into same place as last sl st, inserting hook from back to front work 1dc around stem of next dc — 1dc back worked —, 1dc back into next dc, *(1dc, ch1, 1dc) into next 1ch sp, 1dc back into each of next 2dc, rep from * 4 times more, (1dc, ch1, 1dc) into last 1ch sp, 1dc back around first 3ch of 1st round, 1dc back around first dc of 1st round, sl st to 3rd of first 4ch. 24dc.

3rd round Sl st into first 1ch sp, ch4 to count as first dc and 1ch sp, 1dc into same 1ch sp, *1dc back into each of next 4dc, (1dc, ch1, 1dc) into next 1ch sp, rep from * 4 times more, 1dc back into each of next 4 sts, sl st to 3rd of first 4ch. 36dc.

Cont to inc 12dc on each round as set, working 1dc back into each dc on sides and (1dc, ch1, 1dc) into each 1ch sp at corners.

Patterns and alternatives

2

2 Simple octagon

Ch 5, sl st to first ch to form a circle.
1st round Ch 3 to count as first dc, 15dc into circle, sl st to 3rd of first 3ch. 16 sts.
2nd round Ch 3 to count as first dc, 2dc at base of 3ch, *1dc into next dc, 3dc into next dc, rep from * 6 times more, 1dc into next dc, sl st to 3rd of first 3ch. 32 sts.
3rd round Ch 3 to count as first dc, *3dc into next dc. 1dc into each of next 3dc, rep from * 6 times more, 3dc into next dc, 1dc into each of next 2dc, sl st to 3rd of first 3ch. 48 sts.
4th round Ch 3 to count as first dc, 1dc into next dc, *3dc into next dc, 1dc into each of next 5dc, rep from * 6 times more, 3dc into next dc, 1dc into each of next 3dc, sl st to 3rd of first 3ch. 64 sts. Cont to inc 16 sts on each round as set, working 3dc into dc at each corner.

Note: This shape can be worked in one color or in stripes as here.

3 Flower hexagon

Ch 6, sl st to first ch to form a circle.
1st round Ch 3, leaving last loop of each dc on hook work 2dc into circle, yo and draw through all 3 loops on hook — 2dc cluster formed —, *ch3, leaving last loop of each dc on hook work 3dc into circle, yo and draw through all 4 loops on hook — 3dc cluster worked —, rep from * 4 times more, ch1, 1hdc into top of 2dc cluster. 6 clusters.
2nd round Ch 3, 2dc cluster into side of hdc just worked, *ch3, (3dc cluster, ch3, 3dc cluster) into next 3ch loop, rep from * ending 3ch, 3dc into top of hdc on previous round, ch1, 1hdc into 3rd of first 3ch. 12 clusters.
3rd round Ch 3 to count as first dc, 2dc cluster into top of hdc just worked, *ch3, (3dc cluster, ch3, 3dc cluster) into next 3ch loop, ch3, 3dc cluster into next 3ch loop, rep from * 4 times, ch3, (3dc cluster, ch3, 3dc cluster) into next 3ch loop, ch1, 1hdc into 3rd of first 3ch. 18 clusters.

4th round Ch 3, 1dc into side of hdc just worked, 2dc into next 3ch loop, *(2dc ch2, 2dc) into next 3ch loop, (2dc into next 3ch loop) twice, rep from * 4 times, (2dc, ch2, 2dc) into next 3ch loop, sl st to 3rd of first 3ch. 48dc.
5th round Ch 3 to count as first dc, 1dc into each of next 5dc, *3dc into next 2ch sp, 1dc into each of next 8dc, rep from * 4 times more, 3dc into next 2ch sp, 1dc into each of next 2dc, sl st to top of first 3ch. 66dc.
6th round Ch 3 to count as first dc, 1dc into each of next 6dc, *3dc into next dc, 1dc into each of next 10dc, rep from * 4 times more, 3dc into next dc, 1dc into each of next 3dc, sl st to top of first 3ch. 78dc.
Cont to inc 12dc on each round as set, working 3dc into each dc at corner.

3

Frilly pillows

Unashamedly pretty and feminine pillows give a special touch to a bedroom. One is petaled, the other ruffled.

Petal pillow

Size
Approx 15in in diameter

Materials
Approx 500yds of a size 3 crochet cotton
Size C crochet hook
½yd lining material, 36in wide
Pillow form 15in in diameter

Note: See Working around the stem on page 149.

Front
Using size C hook, ch8, sl st to first ch to form a ring.
1st round Ch 6, 1dc into ring, *ch3, 1dc into ring, rep from * 3 times more, ch3, sl st to 3rd of 6ch. 6sp.

2nd round *Into next loop work 1sc, 1hdc, 3dc, 1hdc, 1sc, rep from * 5 times more.
3rd round Ch 5, *working into back, make 1sc around stem of next dc of first round, ch5, rep from * 4 times more, join with sl st to first sc.
4th round *Into 5ch sp work 1sc, 1hdc, 5dc, 1hdc, 1sc, rep from * to end.
5th round *Ch 7, 1sc into back of sc between petals of previous round, rep from * 4 times more, ch7, join with sl st to first ch of first 7ch.
6th round *Into 7ch loop work 1sc, 1hdc, 7dc, 1hdc, 1sc, rep from * to end.
7th round *Ch 9, 1sc into back of sc between petals of previous round, rep from * 4 times more, ch9, join with sl st to first ch of first 9ch.

8th round *Into 9ch loop work 1sc, 1hdc, 9dc, 1hdc, 1sc, rep from * to end.
9th round *Ch11, 1sc into back of sc between petals of previous round, rep from * 4 times more, ch11, join with sl st to first ch of first 11ch.
10th round *Into 11ch loop work 1sc, 1hdc, 11dc, 1hdc, 1sc, rep from * to end.
11th round *Ch 5, 1sc between 5th and 6th dc of previous round, ch5, 1sc into back of sc between petals of previous round, rep from * 5 times more, omitting last sc, join with sl st to first ch of first 5ch. 12 loops.
12th – 19th rounds As 4th–11th, working the additional number of repeats.
20th – 26th rounds As 4th–10th, working the additional number of repeats.
27th and 28th rounds As 9th and 10th, working additional number of repeats.
Rep last 2 rounds once more.
31st round As 9th, working additional repeats.
32nd round (picot round) *Into 11ch loop work 1sc, 1hdc, 6dc, 3ch, sl st into first of 3ch — called 1 picot —, 6dc, 1hdc, 1sc, rep from * to end.
33rd round As 9th, working additional repeats.
34th round (picot round) *Into 11ch loop work 1sc, 1hdc, 1dc, 5tr, 1 picot, 5tr, 1dc, 1hdc, 1sc, rep from * to end.
Rep last 2 rounds once more. Fasten off.

Back
Using size C hook, ch4, sl st to first ch to form a ring.

The surface crochet technique using a contrast color on the second row of the ruffle.

Patterns and alternatives

1st round Work 8sc into ring, join with sl st to first sc.

2nd round Ch 4, 1dc into same place as sl st, *into next sc work 1ch, 1dc, 1ch, 1dc, rep from * to end, ch1, join with sl st to 3rd of 4ch. 16dc.

3rd round Sl st into first sp, ch4, 1dc into same sp, *into next sp work 1ch, 1dc, 1ch, 1dc, rep from * to end, ch1, join with sl st to 3rd of 4ch.

4th round Sl st into first sp, ch4, *1dc into next sp, ch1, rep from * to end, join with sl st to 3rd of 4ch.

5th round As 3rd.

6th–9th rounds As 4th.

10th and 11th rounds Sl st into first sp, ch5, *1dc into next sp, ch2, rep from * to end, join with sl st to 3rd of 5ch.

12th and 13th rounds Sl st into first sp, ch6, *1dc into next sp, ch3, rep from * to end, join with sl st to 3rd of 6ch.

14th and 15th rounds Sl st into first sp, ch7, *1dc into next sp, ch4, rep from * to end, join with sl st to 3rd of 7ch.

16th round Into each 4ch sp work 4sc. Fasten off.

To finish

Fold lining material in half and cut out two circles 16in in diameter. With right sides together, stitch ½in from the edge, leaving an opening of about 10in. Trim seam allowance and turn right side out. Insert pillow form and, using matching sewing thread, slipstitch opening closed.

With right sides together, hand stitch the pillow Back to Front, leaving an opening of about 10in. Turn right side out, insert pillow form and slipstitch opening closed.

Ruffled pillow

Size

Approx 15in in diameter

Materials

Approx 560yds of size 3 crochet cotton
Size C crochet hook
½yd lining material, 36in wide
Pillow form 15in in diameter

Front

Using size C hook, ch4, sl st to first ch to form a ring.

1st round Work 8sc into ring, join with sl st to first sc.

2nd round *Ch6, 1sc into next sc, rep from * 6 times more, ch3, 1dc into last sc. 8 loops.

3rd round *Ch 3, 1sc into next 6ch loop, rep from * to end, 1sc into dc.

4th round *Ch 6, 1sc into next sc, ch6, 1sc into next 3ch loop, ch6, 1sc into next sc, rep from * until two 3ch loops rem, ch6, 1sc into next sc, ch6, 1sc into next 3ch loop, ch3, 1dc into first ch of first 6ch.

Rep 3rd and 4th rounds 4 times more, then 3rd round once.

14th round *Ch6, 1sc into next sc, rep from * to end, ch3, 1dc into first ch of first 6 ch.

Rep 3rd and 14th rounds 3 times more, then 3rd round once. Fasten off.

Ruffles

Starting at center and working outwards, join yarn to any 6ch loop on the 2nd round, *work 6sc into 6ch loop taking yarn around ch and not into it, rep from * to end of round. Join with sl st to first sc. Fasten off.

Join yarn to any 6ch loop on 4th round and work 8sc into each 6ch loop as before.

Work as for 4th round on 6th and every alt round.

Rejoin yarn to first ruffle and work 1sc into each sc. Join with sl st to first sc and fasten off.

Work a second layer to each ruffle in the same way.

Back

Work as given for Back of Petal pillow.

To finish

Finish as given for Petal pillow but join Back and Front of crochet cover by placing wrong sides together and working sc through the double thickness.

Berry stitch cushions

**It takes very little time to make these attractive cushions,
and they provide comfortable and portable seating
whenever — and wherever — you need it.**

Size
Approx 14in square and 1in deep

Gauge
6 sts to 2in over front pat worked on
size I hook
To save time, check your gauge.

Materials
8oz of knitting worsted or double
knitting yarn
Size I crochet hook
Piece of foam rubber measuring
14in × 14in × 1in

Note: See Working a berry stitch on
page 155.

Front
Using size I hook, ch48.
Base row 1sc into 2nd ch from hook,
1sc into each ch to end. 48 sts.
1st row (WS) Ch 1, skip first sc, sl st
into next st, *yo, insert hook into next
st, yo and draw through a loop, yo and
draw through first loop on hook (3
loops on hook), yo, insert hook into
same st, yo and draw through first 4
loops on hook (2 loops on hook), yo and

draw through 2 loops on hook — called
Berry 1 or B1 —, sl st into next st, rep
from * to last 2 sts, B1 into next st, 1sc
into turning ch. Turn.
2nd row Ch 1, skip first sc, 1 sl st into
each berry st and 1sc into each sl st to
end, ending 1sc into turning ch.
Turn.
3rd row Ch 1, skip first dc, *B1 into
next st, sl st into next st, rep from * to
last st, 1sc into turning ch. Turn.
4th row Ch 1, skip first sc, 1sc into
each sl st and 1 sl st into each berry st
to end, ending 1sc into turning ch.
Turn.
1st—4th rows form pat. Rep pat until
work measures approx 13¼in from
beg, ending with a 2nd row.
Fasten off.

Back
Using size I hook, ch49.
Base row 1hdc into 3rd ch from hook,
1hdc into each ch to end. Turn. 48 sts.
Pat row Ch 2, skip first hdc, 1hdc into
each hdc, 1hdc into top of turning ch.
Turn. Rep pat row until work measures
same as front.
Fasten off.

To finish
With right sides together, overcast
back to front on three sides. Turn right
side out. Insert foam pad and overcast
the opening to close it.

Alternatives
**Use several of these berry
stitch patterns to make a set of
beautifully textured cushions
for comfortable seating indoors
and out.**

Berry stitch patterns are particularly
effective for cushions and pillows
because they provide a firm fabric
which is pleasant to the touch but firm
enough to withstand wear and tear.
Choose an easily washable, hard-
wearing yarn. A good-looking mixture
of synthetic fibers and wool is ideal.
Unless the back of the cushion is
important, work in a plain stitch such as
single crochet or half double. Using
elaborate stitches would waste yarn.
For flat, box cushions, foam pads are
best. For really plump scatter pillows,
make an inner pad from a closely
woven cotton fabric and fill it with
feathers or synthetic batting.

Other uses
Since berry stitch patterns are worked
on a background of single crochet, they
produce a firm, neat fabric which is
useful not only for cushions and pillows
but also for other household
accessories such as bathmats or
bedspreads. Most articles worked in
single crochet can be adapted to berry
stitch patterns, but the gauge may
change slightly when the berries are
introduced.
Use berry stitches either as an allover
pattern or as blocks of texture on a
single crochet background. When used
as an allover pattern, crochet berry
stitch resembles the trinity stitch used
in Aran knitting. Berry stitch panels
can add an interesting, Aran-look
texture to otherwise plain fabric.

2 Dotted berry pattern

Make a multiple of 4ch plus 4 extra.
Base row 1sc into 2nd ch from hook,
1sc into each ch to end. Turn.
1st row (WS) Ch 1, 1sc into first sc,
(1 berry st into next sc, 1sl st into next
sc, 1sc into each of next 2sc) to last
2sc, 1 berry st into next sc, 1sc into
last sc. Turn.
2nd row Ch 1, 1sc into each st ending
1sc into last sc. Turn.
3rd row Ch 1, 1sc into each of first
3sc, (1 berry st into next sc, 1sl st into
next sc, 1sc into each of next 2sc) to
end. Turn.
4th row As 2nd.
1st–4th rows form pat. Rep them
throughout, ending with a 2nd or 4th
row.

Berry stitch patterns

1 Vertical berry pattern

Make a multiple of 5ch plus 1 extra.
Base row 1sc into 2nd ch from hook,
1sc into each ch to end. Turn.
1st row (WS) Ch1, 1sc into each of
first 2sc, (1 berry st into next sc, 1sl st
into next sc, 1sc into each of next 3sc)
to last 3sc, 1 berry st into next sc, 1sl
st into next sc, 1sc into last sc. Turn.
2nd row Ch 1, 1sc into first sc, 1sc
into each st ending 1sc into last sc.
Turn.
1st and 2nd rows form pat. Rep them
throughout.

2

1

3 Chevron berry pattern

Make a multiple of 8ch plus 4 extra.
Base row 1sc into 2nd ch from hook,
1sc into each ch to end. Turn.
1st row (WS) Ch 1, 1sc into first sc,
(1 berry st into next sc, 1sc into each
of next 7sc) to last 2sc, 1 berry st
into next sc, 1sc into last sc. Turn.
2nd and every alt row Ch 1, 1sc into
first sc, 1sc into each st ending 1sc into
last dc. Turn.
3rd row Ch 1, 1 sc into first sc, 1sc
into each of next 2sc, (1 berry st into
next sc, 1sc into each of next 3sc) to
end. Turn.

5th row Ch 1, 1sc into first sc, (1sc into each of next 4sc, 1 berry st into next sc, 1sc into each of next 3sc) to last 2sc, 1sc into each of last 2sc. Turn.
6th row As 2nd row.
1st–6th rows form pat. Rep them throughout.

5 Striped uneven berry pattern

Make a multiple of 2ch plus 2 extra. Use 2 colors, A and B.
Base row With A, 1sc into 2nd ch from hook, 1sc into each ch to end. Turn.

1st row (WS) With A, ch1, 1sc into first sc, (1 berry st into next st, 1 sl st into next st) to last 2 sts, 1 berry st into next st, 1sc into last sc. Drop A, change to B. Turn.
2nd row With B, ch1, 1sc into first sc, (1 sl st into next berry st, 1sc into next sl st) to last 2 sts, 1 sl st into last berry st, 1sc into last sc. Turn.
3rd row With B, ch1, 1sc into each of first 2 sts, (1 berry st into next st, 1 sl st into next st) to last sc, 1sc into last sc. Drop B, change to A. Turn.
4th row With A, ch1, 1sc into first sc, (1sc into next sc, 1 sl st into next berry st) to last 2 sts, 1sc into each of last 2sc.
1st–4th rows form pat. Rep them throughout.

4 Diamond berry pattern

Make a multiple of 8ch plus 4 extra.
Base row 1sc into 2nd ch from hook, 1sc into each ch to end. Turn.
1st row (WS) Ch 1, 1sc into first sc, (1 berry st into next sc, 1sc into each of next 7sc) to last 2sc, 1 berry st into next sc, 1sc into last sc. Turn.
2nd and every alt row Ch 1, 1sc into first sc, 1sc into each st, ending 1sc into last sc. Turn.
3rd row Ch 1, 1sc into first sc, 1sc into each of next 2sc, (1 berry st into next sc, 1sc into each of next 3sc) to end. Turn.
5th row Ch 1, 1sc in first sc, (1sc in each of next 4sc, 1 berry st in next sc, 1sc into each of next 3sc) to last 2sc, 1sc in each of last 2sc. turn.
7th row As 3rd row.
8th row As 2nd row.
1st–8th rows form pat. Rep them throughout.

Table linen

Crossed inlay tablecloth

Lacy crochet squares worked in fine cotton are sewn to
linen squares to make this attractive cloth.

Patterns and alternatives

Size
Cloth measures approx 26in square

Gauge
1 crochet square measures approx 2in square
To save time, check your gauge.

Materials
Approx 535yds of a size 20 crochet cotton
No 8 steel crochet hook
4 pieces linen approx 12in square each
Matching thread

Note: See Working in fine cotton on page 14 and Working an open center on page 150.

1st square
Wind crochet cotton 12 times around end of pencil, slip off and catch ring together with a sl st.
1st round Ch 3, 2dc into ring, ch7, (3dc, ch7) 7 times into ring. Join with a sl st to 3rd of first 3ch.
2nd round Sl st across next 2dc and 2ch, ch3, keeping last loop of each st on hook, work 3dc into first 7ch loop, yo and through all loops on hook — called 3dc cluster —, (ch9, leaving last loop of each st on hook, work 4dc into next 7ch loop, yo and through all loops on hook — called 4dc cluster —,) 7 times, ch9. Join with a sl st to top of first cluster.
3rd round *(2sc, ch5, 2sc) into next 9ch loop, ch7, (4dc cluster, ch5, 4dc cluster) into next 9ch loop, ch7, rep from * to end of round. Join with a sl st to first sc.
4th round Sl st into next sc and into 5ch loop, 2sc into same loop, *ch5, 2sc into next 7ch loop, ch5, (4dc cluster, ch5, 4dc cluster) into next 5ch loop, ch5, 2sc into next 7ch loop, ch5, 2sc into next 5ch loop, rep from * to end of round ending with 5ch, join with a sl st to beg of round.
Fasten off.

2nd square
Work first 3 rounds as given for 1st square.
4th round (joining round) Sl st into next sc and into 5ch loop, 2sc into same loop, ch5, 2sc into next 7ch loop, ch5, 4dc cluster into next 5ch loop, ch2, sl st to corner 5ch loop of 1st square, ch2, 4dc cluster into same 5ch loop of 2nd square, (ch2, sl st to next loop of 1st square, ch2, 2sc into next loop of 2nd square 3 times, ch2, sl st into next loop of 1st square, ch2, 4dc cluster into next loop of 2nd square, ch2, sl st into corner loop of 1st square, ch2, 4dc cluster into same loop of 2nd square.

Now complete 2nd square as given for 1st square.
Cont working squares in this way, joining each square while working the last round.
Work one strip of 11 squares and 2 strips of 5 squares each.
Join these strips to form a cross.

To finish
Press both the linen and crochet under a damp cloth, pinning crochet out to shape before pressing. Turn and baste a hem all around linen so that each piece measures 10¾in square.
With RS of linen facing and using size 8 steel crochet hook, work close single crochet over fold, inserting hook through both layers of fabric at each stitch.
When hems have been completed cut away excess fabric on WS.
Sew the crochet squares to the single crochet border on hem, using matching thread.

Special technique — edging the fabric

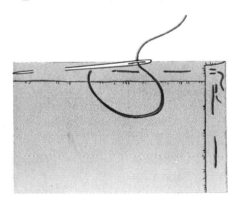

1 *Turn a single hem to the wrong side of the fabric all around and baste it in place making sure that all pieces of fabric to be used are the same size. Clip the corners diagonally if you are using thick fabric.*

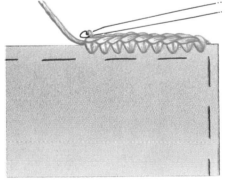

2 *With RS of the fabric facing, insert the fine hook firmly through both layers of fabric and work single crochet stitches closely along the edge of the material. Work from right to left making sure that the stitches are worked evenly so that the fabric is not pulled out of shape.*

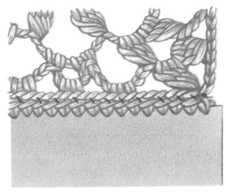

3 *With the RS of the fabric up and the fabric and crochet side by side, sew the crochet square to the single crochet edging on the fabric using a matching sewing thread.*

Lace edging

1st round With RS of work facing, join yarn to sc at any corner, ch3, 3dc cluster into same sc as join, ch5, 4dc cluster into next sc, *ch5, skip ¼in along edge, 1sc into each of next 2sc, ch5, skip ¼in along edge, 4dc cluster into next sc, ch5, 4dc cluster into next sc, rep from * ending with 2sc at corner before square. Work across square as follows: ch5, skip corner loop of motif, (4dc cluster, ch5, 4dc cluster) into next loop, (ch5, 2sc into next loop) twice, ch5, (4dc cluster, ch5, 4dc cluster) into next loop, ch5, 2sc into corner of next square of cloth, ch5, cont in pat to match edging already worked. Join final 5ch to top of first cluster with a sl st.

2nd round Sl st into 5ch loop, ch3, 3dc cluster into same loop, ch5, 4dc cluster into same loop, *(ch5, 2sc into next loop) twice, ch5, (4dc cluster, ch5, 4dc cluster) into next loop, rep from * all around cloth but working an extra 5ch loop at center of square to keep pat correct.
Join final 5ch to top of first cluster with a sl st.
Fasten off.
Press completed cloth on WS under a damp cloth.

Note: Washing may cause crochet to lose its shape. Pin the cloth to correct size and press firmly under a damp cloth.

Alternatives

Many individual motifs, including those featured below, can be combined with fabric to make elegant household accessories.

The technique of combining fabric with crochet squares or strips was used extensively during the nineteenth century to decorate household linen, baby clothes and underwear. The crochet was usually worked in white or ecru cotton and combined with fine white linen. With the advent of colored crochet cottons and fabric dyes and the availability of so many different

1

materials, it is possible to bring this technique up to date and make attractive items suitable for the most modern of homes.

Different shapes and ideas

Squares, rectangles and straight pieces of fabric can all be trimmed with crochet to make not only tablecloths but also place mats, napkins and tray cloths. A crochet insertion in a matching color near the lower edge of a simple cotton curtain or blind makes an attractive window decoration and contrasting cotton squares joined with crochet strips can be turned into a pretty bedspread. Other shapes such as circles and ovals can be used too. By placing a single crochet circle in the center of a circular piece of fabric and edging the fabric with a simple crochet border you can make a round tablecloth. Several rounds could be used as insertions around the lower edge of a circular tablecloth, or joined to become the center of an otherwise plain round cloth.

The best results are obtained by using a fine or medium weight crochet cotton for the squares or rounds. They are firm enough to hold the shape of the

crochet without being too heavy for the fabric. Threads that are too heavy can pull the fabric out of shape.

For the fabric, good quality, loosely woven cotton and firm linen are suitable because they hold the crochet shapes firmly. A heavier fabric will overpower the crochet and spoil the effect of using fabric and crochet together.

Directions for joining the crochet squares used in our tablecloth are given on page 50. If you select a different pattern, you can either overcast the crochet squares together with a matching sewing thread or create your own joining by working chain loops along the sides of the squares to be joined and attaching the squares with slip stitches between the loops.

Inlaid motif patterns

1 Arched square

Ch 8. Sl st into first ch to form a circle.
1st round Ch 3, 2dc into ring, ch7, (3dc, 7ch) 7 times into ring. Join with a sl st to top of 3ch at beg of round.
2nd round Sl st into next 7ch loop, ch3, 2dc into same loop, ch2, 3dc into

same loop, *ch7, skip next loop, (3dc, ch2, 3dc) into next loop, rep from * twice more, ch7, skip last loop. Join with a sl st to top of first 3ch.

3rd round Ch 3, 1dc into each of next 2dc, *(2dc, ch2, 2dc) into corner space, 1dc into each of next 3dc, ch7, 1dc into each of next 3dc, rep from * twice more, (2dc, ch2, 2dc) into corner space. 1dc into each of next 3dc, ch7. Join with a sl st to top of first 3ch.

4th round Ch 3, 1dc into each of next 4dc, *(2dc, ch2, 2dc) into corner space, 1dc into each of next 5dc, ch4, 1sc into skipped 7ch loop of 1st round

and enclosing chains of 2nd and 3rd rounds, ch4, 1dc into each of next 5dc, rep from * 3 times more, omitting last 5dc. Join with a sl st to top of first 3ch. Fasten off.

2 Openwork square

Ch 6, sl st into first chain to form a circle.

1st round Ch 5, (6dc into ring, ch2) 3 times, 5dc into ring. Join with a sl st into 5ch space.

2nd round Ch 5, 3dc into same space as sl st, *ch5, (3dc, ch2, 3dc) into next 2ch space, rep from * twice more, ch5, 2dc into same space as 3dc at beg of round. Join with a sl st into 5ch space at beg of round.

3rd round Ch 5, 3dc into same space as sl st, *ch5, 1sc into 5ch space, ch5, (3dc, ch2, 3dc) into corner 2ch space, rep from * twice more, ch5, 1sc, ch5, 2dc into same space as 3dc at beg. Join with a sl st into 5ch space.

4th round Work as 3rd, but working an extra 5ch, 1sc, on each side of square.

5th round Ch5, 3 dc into same space as sl st, *ch5, 1sc into next 5ch space, 6 dc into next 5ch space, 1 sc into following 5ch space, ch5, (3dc, ch2, 3dc) into corner 2ch space, rep from * twice more, ch5, 1sc into next space, 6dc into next space, 1sc into following space, ch5, 2dc into same space as 3dc at beg of round. Join with a sl st into 5ch space.
Fasten off.

3 Ornate square

Use 2 colors, A and B.
Using A, ch6, sl st to first chain to form a circle.

1st round Ch 5, (6dc into ring, ch2) 3 times, 5dc into ring. Join with a sl st to 3rd of first 5ch. Fasten off.

2nd round Using B, join yarn to any 2ch space, (2sc into 2ch space, ch10) 4 times. Join with a sl st to beg of round.

3rd round (1sc into each sc, 15sc into 10ch loop) 4 times. Join with a sl st to beg of round.

4th round Sl st into each of next 5sc, (1sc into each of next 9sc, ch7, skip next 8sc) 4 times. Join with a sl st to beg of round.

5th round Sl st into next sc, (1sc into each of next 7sc, ch5, 2sc into 7ch loop, ch5, sl st to top of last dc, 1dc into 7ch loop, ch5, skip next sc) 4 times. Join with a sl st to beg of round. Fasten off.

4 Two-color rosette

Use 2 colors, A and B.
Using A, wind yarn 20 times around tip of little finger. Catch the ring tog with a sl st.

1st round Work 24sc into ring. Join with a sl st to beg of round.

2nd round (ch20, skip 1sc, 1sc into each of next 2sc) 8 times. Join with a sl st to beg of round. Fasten off.

3rd round Using A, join yarn to center of any 20ch loop, 2sc into same loop, (ch10, 2sc into next loop) 7 times, ch10. Join with a sl st to beg of round.

4th round Sl st into next sc and into 10ch loop, ch3, 15dc into same loop, (16dc into next loop) 7 times.

5th round (1sc into first st of next group, 1dc in each of next 14dc, 1sc into last st of group) 8 times. Join with sl st to beg of round. Fasten off.

6th round Using B, work as for 5th round.

7th round Work (2 loose sc inserting hook into space between doubles of 4th round, 1dc into each of next 14dc) 8 times. Join with a sl st to beg of round.
Fasten off.

3

4

5 Two-color wheel

Use two colors, A and B.

Using A, ch6. Sl st into first chain to form a circle.

1st round Work 16sc into ring. Join with a sl st to first sc.

2nd round Ch 12, *1dtr into next sc, ch2, 1dtr into following sc, ch6, rep form * 6 times more, 1dtr into next sc, ch2. Join with a sl st to 6th of first 12ch. Fasten off.

3rd round Using B, join yarn to any

6ch space, 2sc into same space, *ch5, leaving last loop of each st on hook work 4dc into next 2ch space, yo and through all loops on hook — called 4dc cluster —, ch5, 2sc into next 6ch space, rep from * all around, omitting last 2sc and ending with one sl st to sc at beginning of round. Fasten off.

6 Floral ring

Wind yarn 20 times around tip of little finger. Catch ring tog with a sl st.

1st round Ch 4, 4tr into ring, (ch2, 5tr into ring) 5 times, ch2. Join with a sl st to top of first 4ch.

2nd round Ch 4, leaving last loop of each st on hook work 4tr over next 4tr, yo and through all loops on hook — called 4tr cluster —, (ch6, 1dc into next 2ch space, ch6, leaving last loop of each st on hook work 5tr over next 5tr, yo and through all loops on hook — called 5tr cluster —,) 5 times, ch6, 1dc into next 2ch space, ch6. Join with a sl st to top of first cluster.

3rd round Sl st to center of next 6ch, 2sc into same loop, *ch7, 2sc into center of next 6ch loop, rep from * all around. Join with a sl st to first sc.

4th round Sl st into next 7ch loop, ch3, leaving last loop of each st on hook work 3dc into same loop, yo and through all loops on hook — called 3dc cluster —, *ch9, leaving last loop of each st on hook work 4dc into same loop, yo and through all loops on hook — called 4dc cluster —, 4dc cluster into next loop, rep from * all around, ending with ch9, 4dc cluster into last loop. Join with a sl st to top of first cluster. Fasten off.

7 Catherine wheel

Wind yarn 20 times around tip of little finger. Catch ring tog with a sl st.

1st round Work 21sc into ring. Join with a sl st to first sc.

1st "arm" Ch 10, fasten a safety-pin to 10th ch, work 20sc back over 10ch, sl st into next sc of 1st round, turn, (ch4, skip 4sc, 1sc into next sc) 4 times, turn, (6sc into next 4ch loop) 4 times, skip next sc on 1st round. Join with a sl st to following sc. Turn.

2nd "arm" Ch 10, sl st to center of 2nd loop from center, turn, work 20sc

6

into 10ch loop, sl st into next sc of 1st round, complete "arm" as before. Work 5 more "arms" and join last to the first with a sl st into place marked with a safety-pin; i.e. working (3sc, sl st, 3sc) into 4ch loop instead of 6sc.

7

5

Wheatear mat and coasters

Edge a piece of linen with fine crochet in a crisp wheatear
pattern. Work coasters to match and you have a set that will
add elegance to any table setting.

Sizes

Edged place mat measures approx
14¼in in diameter
Coaster measures approx 4¾in in
diameter

Gauge

Edging measures 1¼in in depth
To save time, check your gauge.

Materials

Approx 350yds of a size 20 crochet
cotton
(approx 175yds for one edging and one
coaster)
Size 8 steel crochet hook
Circle of linen approx 13¾in in
diameter

Note: See Working a chainless base on
page 151 and Working in fine cotton on
page 14.

Special abbreviations

Wg — wheatgrain ** yo twice,
insert hook into st, yo and draw
through a loop, (yo and draw through
first 2 loops on hook) twice**, rep from
** to ** 3 times more, yo and draw
through all five loops on hook.

Note: At beg of rows or rounds work
wg as foll: ch4, rep from ** to ** 3
times in all, yo and draw through all 4
loops on hook.

Coaster (make 4)

Using size 8 steel hook, ch8, sl st to
first ch to form a circle.
1st round Ch 3, 1dc into circle, ch4,
(work 2dc tog, ch4) 7 times into circle,
sl st to top of first 3ch. 8 4ch-sps.
2nd round Sl st into next 4ch sp, ch4,
1tr into same place as sl st, ch6, (work
2tr tog into next 4ch sp, ch6) 7 times,
sl st to top of first 4ch. 8 6ch-sps.

3rd round Ch6, 1tr into same place as
sl st, ch3, 1tr into next 6ch sp, ch3,
*(1tr, ch2, 1tr) into top of next 2tr tog,
3ch, 1tr into next 6ch sp, ch3, rep from
* 6 times more, sl st to 4th of first 6ch.
4th round * (wg, ch2, 1dc, ch2, wg)
into next 2ch sp, ch5, skip next 3ch sp,
1tr into next tr, ch5, skip next 3ch sp,
rep from * 7 times more, sl st into first
2ch sp.
5th round * wg into next 2ch sp, ch2,
1dc into next dc, ch2, wg into next 2ch
sp, ch4, (1tr, ch2, 1tr) into next tr,
ch4, rep from * 7 times more, sl st into
first 2ch sp.
6th round * wg into next 2ch sp, ch2,
1dc into next dc, ch2, wg into next 2ch
sp, ch3, skip next 4ch sp, (wg, ch2,
1dc, ch2, wg) into next 2ch sp, ch3,
skip next 4ch sp, rep from * 7 times
more, sl st into first 2ch sp.
7th round (wg into next 2ch sp, ch2,
1dc into next dc, ch2, wg into next 2ch
sp, ch4) 16 times, sl st into first 2ch sp.
8th round Sl st into top of next dc, wg
into same place as sl st, ch7, (1sc, ch3,
1sc) into next 4ch loop, ch7, *wg into
next dc, ch7, (1sc, ch3, 1sc) into next
4ch loop, ch7, rep from * 14 times
more, sl st to top of wg. Fasten off.

Mat edging

Using size 8 steel hook, ch4.
Base 1dc into 4th ch from hook, *ch3,
1dc into sp between previous dc and
ch, rep from * 169 times more, sl st
into first sp to form a circle, making
sure that work is not twisted. 171 sps.
1st round (wg, ch2, 1dc, ch2, wg) into
same sp as sl st, *ch3, skip next 2 sps,
(wg, ch2, 1dc, ch2, wg) into next sp,
rep from * to end, ending with 3ch, sl
st into first 2ch sp. 57 pairs of wg.
2nd round Wg into same place as sl
st, ch2, 1dc into next dc, ch2, wg into
next 2ch sp, *ch4, wg into next 2ch sp,

ch2, 1dc into next dc, ch2, wg into next
2ch sp, rep from * to end, ending with
4ch, sl st into first 2ch sp.
3rd round As 2nd round, but work 5ch
instead of 4ch between each pair of wg.
4th round Sl st into first dc, wg into
same dc, *ch7, (1sc, ch3, 1sc) into
next 5ch sp, ch7, wg into next dc, rep
from * to end, ending with 7ch, (1sc,
ch3, 1sc) into last 5ch sp, ch7, sl st to
top of wg. Fasten off.

To finish

Pin coasters and edging to correct size.
Spray lightly with water and leave to
dry naturally.
Using a soft pencil, draw a circle 11¾in
in diameter on the linen.
Using a contrast-colored thread, baste
along the pencil line.
Using zigzag stitches, machine stitch
the linen just outside the basted line to
prevent fraying. Baste the edging to
the linen so that the inner edge of the
crochet just touches the basted line and
overlaps the machine zigzag.
Using matching yarn, hand-sew the
edging neatly to the linen.
Cut away surplus linen close to the
machine stitching. Remove basting.
Press linen with a hot iron over a damp
cloth, avoiding crochet.

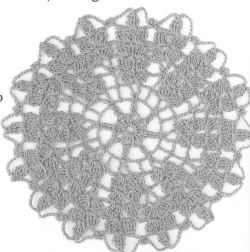

Alternatives

Harvest a crop of alternative grain patterns and use them not only for place mats and coasters but for other household accessories too.

Any of the alternative grain edgings could be substituted for the wheat edging on page 54. Each edging has a matching coaster so you can make a matching set if you wish.

The edgings and coasters could also be used in other ways. The edgings could be used to trim any circular mat or tablecloth. And sewn together, the coasters would make a beautiful, lacy curtain or tablecloth. Use the first few rounds of the coaster to fill any gaps between large circles. The edging could be used to trim the work. These delicate patterns based on wheat and other grains should be worked in fine cotton with a steel hook to help maintain an even gauge; see working in fine cotton on page 14.

Grain patterns

1 Corn

See note on special abbreviations, page 54.

Coaster Ch 8, sl st to first ch to form a circle.

1st round Ch 5, (1tr, ch1) 23 times into circle, sl st to 4th of first 5ch. 24 1ch sps.

2nd round 1sc into sp made by 5th ch, (ch4, 1sc into next 1ch sp) 23 times, ch2, 1dc into first sc.

3rd round (Ch4, 1sc into next 4ch sp) 23 times, ch2, 1dc into top of last dc.

4th round (Ch5, 1sc into next 4ch sp) 23 times, ch2, 1dc into top of last dc.

5th round Ch 5, wg into sp formed by last dc and 2ch, *ch4, skip next 5ch sp, (wg, ch2, 1dc, ch2, wg) into next 5ch sp, rep from * to end, ending with 4ch, wg into first sp, ch2, sl st to 3rd of first 5ch.

6th round Ch 5, wg into first 2ch sp, *

ch4, 1sc into next 4ch sp, ch4, wg into next 2ch sp, ch2, 1dc into next dc, ch2, wg into next 2ch sp, rep from * to end, ending with wg into last 2ch sp, ch2, sl st to 3rd of first 5ch.

7th round Ch5, wg into first 2ch sp, * ch5, wg into next 2ch sp, ch2, 1dc into next dc, ch2, wg into next 2ch sp, rep from * to end, ending with wg into last 2ch sp, sl st to 3rd of first 5ch.

8th round Wg into same place as sl st, *ch7, (1sc, ch3, 1sc) into next 5ch sp, ch7, wg into next dc, rep from * to end, ending with ch7, sl st to top of first wg. Fasten off.

Edging Ch 4.

Base 1tr into 4th ch from hook, *ch4, 1tr into sp between previous tr and 4ch, rep from * for length required, ending with a multiple of 3 sps, sl st into first sp.

1st round (wg, ch2, 1dc, ch2, wg) into same sp, ch4, skip next 2 sps, * (wg, ch2, 1dc, ch2, wg) into next sp, ch4, skip next 2 sps, rep from * to end, ending with sl st into first 2ch sp.

2nd round *wg into next 2ch sp, ch2, 1dc into next dc, ch2, wg into next 2ch sp, ch5, 1sc into next 4ch sp, ch5, rep from * to end, ending with sl st into first 2ch sp.

3rd round *wg into next 2ch sp, ch2, 1dc into next dc, ch2, wg into next 2ch sp, ch5, rep from * to end, ending with sl st into first 2ch sp and into top of dc.

4th round *wg into same dc, ch7, (1sc, ch3, 1sc) into next 5ch sp, ch7, rep from * to end, ending with sl st into top of first wg. Fasten off.

2 Barley

See special abbreviations, page 54.

Coaster Ch 8, sl st to first ch to form a circle.

1st round Ch 3, 1dc into circle, *ch3, work 2dc tog into circle, rep from * 6 times more, ch3, sl st to top of first 3ch.

2nd round Sl st into first 3ch sp, ch4, 1tr into first 3ch sp, *ch6, work 2tr tog into next 3ch sp, rep from * 6 times more, ch6, sl st to top of first 4ch.

3rd round Ch 6, 1tr into same place as sl st, *ch3, 1tr into next 6ch sp, ch3, (1tr, ch2, 1tr) into next 2tr tog, rep from * 6 times more, ch3, 1tr into next 6ch sp, ch3, sl st to 4th of first 6ch.

4th round *(wg, ch2, 1dc, ch2, wg) into next 2ch sp, ch4, 1tr into next tr, 4ch, rep from * 7 times more, sl st into top of first wg.

5th round *wg into next 2ch sp, ch2, 1dc into next dc, ch2, wg into next 2ch sp, ch3, (1tr, ch2, 1tr) into next tr, ch3, rep from * 7 times more, sl st into top of first wg.

6th round *wg into next 2ch sp, ch2, 1dc into next dc, ch2, wg into next 2ch sp, ch4, (1tr, ch2, 1tr, ch2, 1tr) into next 2ch sp, ch4, rep from * 7 times more, sl st into first 2ch sp.

7th round *wg into next 2ch sp, ch2, 1dc into next dc, ch2, wg into next 2ch

1

sp, ch4, 1tr into next tr, ch2, (1tr, ch2, 1tr) into next tr, ch2, 1tr into next tr, ch4, rep from * 7 times more, sl st into first 2ch sp and into next dc.

8th round Wg into same place as sl st, *ch4, (1dc into next tr, ch3, sl st to top of previous dc, ch4) 4 times, wg into next dc, rep from * 7 times more, ending with sl st into top of first wg. Fasten off.

Edging Work base as for Corn, ending with a multiple of 4 sps.

1st round (wg, ch2, 1dc, ch2, wg) into same sp as sl st, ch3, skip next sp, 1tr into next sp, ch3, skip next sp, *(wg, ch2, 1dc, ch2, wg) into next sp, ch3, skip next sp, 1tr into next sp, ch3, skip next sp, rep from * to end, ending with sl st into first 2ch sp.

2nd round *wg into first 2ch sp, ch2, 1dc into next dc, ch2, wg into next 2ch, sp, ch3, (1tr, ch2, 1tr) into next tr, ch3, rep from * to end, ending with sl st into first 2ch sp.

3rd round *wg into first 2ch sp, ch2, 1dc into next dc, ch2, wg into next 2ch sp, ch3, 1tr into next tr, ch2, 1tr into next 2ch sp, ch2, 1tr into next tr, ch3, rep from * to end, ending with sl st into first 2ch sp and into top of first dc.

4th round *wg into same dc, ch3, 1tr into next tr, ch3, sl st to top of last tr, ch3, 1tr into next tr, ch3, sl st to top of last tr, ch3, 1tr into same place as last tr, ch3, sl st to top of last tr, ch3, 1tr into next tr, ch3, sl st to top of last tr, ch3, wg into next dc, rep from * to end,

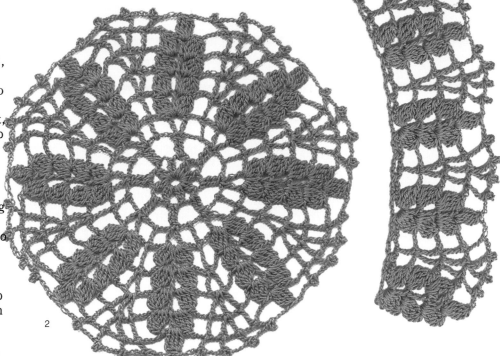

2

omitting last wg and ending with sl st into top of last wg. Fasten off.

3 Rye

See special abbreviations, page 54.
Coaster Work first 3 rounds as for Corn coaster.

4th round As 3rd round.

5th round Ch 5, wg into sp formed by last dc, *ch5, skip next 2 sps, (wg, ch2, 1dc, ch2, wg) into next sp, rep from * all around, ending with wg into sp, ch2, sl st to 3rd of first 5ch.

6th round Ch 5, wg into first 2ch sp, *ch5, (1sc, ch3, 1sc) into next 5ch sp, ch5, wg into next 2ch sp, ch2, 1dc into next dc, ch2, wg into next 2ch sp, rep

from * to end, ending with wg into last 2ch sp, ch2, sl st to 3rd of first 5ch.

7th round Ch 5, wg into first 2ch sp, * (ch5, (1sc, ch3, 1sc) into next 5ch sp) twice, ch5, wg into next 2ch sp, ch2, 1dc into next dc, ch2, wg into next 2ch sp, rep from * to end, ending with wg into last 2ch sp, ch2, sl st to 3rd of first 5ch.

8th round Wg into same place as sl st, *(ch7, 1sc into next sp, ch3, 1sc into same sp) 3 times, ch7, wg into next dc, rep from * to end, ending with sl st to top of first wg. Fasten off.

Edging Work base as for Corn, ending with a multiple of 4 sps.

1st round (wg, ch2, 1dc, ch2, wg) into same sp as sl st, ch5, skip next sp, (1sc, ch3, 1sc) into next sp, ch5, skip next sp, *(wg, ch2, 1dc, ch2, wg) into next sp, ch5, skip next sp, (1sc, ch3, 1sc) into next sp, ch5, skip next sp, rep from * to end, ending with sl st into first 2ch sp.

2nd round *wg into next 2ch sp, ch2, 1dc into next dc, ch2, wg into next 2ch sp, (ch5, (1sc, ch3, 1sc) into next 5ch sp) twice, rep from * to end, ending with sl st into first 2ch sp, sl st into top of first dc.

3rd round *wg into next dc, (ch5, (1sc, ch3, 1sc) into next 5ch sp) 3 times, ch5, rep from * to end, ending with sl st into top of first wg. Fasten off.

3

Rustic mats

These practical, good-looking mats are made from string and twine.

Rectangular place mat

Size
approx 9½in wide by 11¾in long

Gauge
11sc to 4in worked on size I hook
To save time, check your gauge.

Materials
Twine for wrapping packages
Size I crochet hook

Note: See Working continuous rounds, page 151 and Crab stitch edging, page 154.

To make
Using size I hook, ch10.
1st round 1sc into 3rd ch from hook, 1sc into each ch to within last ch, 3sc into last ch. Do not turn but work along other side of foundation ch, 1sc into each ch to end, 3sc into turning ch. Do not join. Working into back loop only of each st work in continuous rounds as follows:
2nd round 1sc into each of next 7sc, 3sc into next sc — corner formed —, 1sc into next sc, 3sc into next sc — corner formed —, 1sc into each of next 7sc, 3sc into next sc — corner formed —, 1sc into next sc, 3sc into next sc — corner formed.
3rd round 1sc into each of next 8sc, 3sc into next sc, 1sc into each of next 3sc, 3sc into next sc, 1sc into each of next 9sc, 3sc into next sc, 1sc into each of next 3sc, 3sc into next sc, 1sc into last sc.
Cont to work in this way, working 1sc into each sc on each side and 3sc into center sc at each corner until 13 rounds in all have been worked and mat measures 8¼in by 11in, ending last round by working a sl st into 1st sc. Work a row of crab stitch (sc worked from left to right), working into both loops of each st all around, sl st into first st. Fasten off. Weight mat for several hours to flatten if necessary.

Octagonal place mat

Size
approx 9½in across

Gauge
12 hdc and 9 rows to 4in on size I hook.

Materials
Fine macrame string
Size I crochet hook

To make
Using size I hook, ch4, sl st into first ch to form a circle.
1st round Ch2 to count as first hdc, 7 hdc into circle, sl st into 2nd of first 2ch. 8hdc.
2nd round Ch2 to count as first hdc, 1hdc into st at base of 2ch, 2hdc into each st all around, sl st into 2nd of first 2ch. 16hdc.
3rd round Ch2, 1hdc into st at base of 2ch, 1hdc into next st, *2hdc into next st, 1hdc into next st, rep from * all around, sl st into 2nd of first 2ch.
4th round Ch 2, 1hdc into st at base of 2ch, 1hdc into each of next 2sts, *2hdc into next st, 1hdc into each of next 2 sts, rep from * all around, sl st into 2nd of first 2ch.
5th round Ch 2, 1hdc into st at base of 2ch, 1hdc into each of next 3sts, *2hdc into next st, 1hdc into each of next 3 sts, rep from * all around, sl st into 2nd of first 2ch. Cont to work in this way, working 1 more st on each side of octagon between increases until there are 8hdc between each increase.
Next round Ch 1 to count as first sc, 1sc into st at base of ch, 1sc into each of next 9 sts, 2sc into next st, 1sc into each of next 9sc, rep from * all around, sl st into first ch. Fasten off.

Floor mat

Size
32½in wide by 37in long

Gauge
8 single crochet to 4in worked on size K hook

Materials
9 balls of thick garden twine
Size K crochet hook

Note: Ball of twine used weighed 8oz

To make
Using size K hook, ch14.
1st round 1sc into 3rd ch from hook, 1sc into each ch to within last ch, 3sc into last ch. Do not turn but work along other side of foundation ch, 1sc into each ch to end, 3sc into turning ch. Do not join. Working into back loop only of each st work in continuous rounds as follows:
2nd round 1sc into each of next 11sc, 3sc into next sc — corner formed —, 1sc into next sc, 3sc into next sc — corner formed —, 1sc into each of next 11sc, 3sc into next sc — corner formed —, 1sc into next sc, 3sc into next sc — corner formed.
3rd round 1sc into each of next 12sc, 3sc into next sc, 1sc into each of next 3sc, 3sc into next sc, 1sc into each of next 13sc, 3sc into next sc, 1sc into each of next 3sc, 3sc into next sc, 1sc into next sc.
Cont to work in this way, working 3sc into center sc at each corner on every round and working extra sc on each side until 76 rounds in all have been worked and mat measures 31½in by 36¼in. Work a row of crab stitch (sc worked from left to right) into back loop of each st all around, sl st into first st. Fasten off. Weight as before.

Snowflake tea cloth

This hexagonal tea cloth is formed by linking delicate snowflake motifs. Use it to cover a tray or a tea or bedside table.

Size
Width at widest points, about 22in

Gauge
Each snowflake shape measures about 2¼in
To save time, check your gauge.

Materials
Approx 885yds of a size 20 crochet cotton
Size 7 steel crochet hook

Note: See Working in fine cotton on page 14.

First motif
Using size 7 steel hook, ch10. Sl st into first ch to form a ring.
1st round Ch 4, (1dc into ring, ch1) 11 times, sl st into 3rd of 4ch.
1st row Ch 13, 1dc into 4th ch from hook, placing hook around length of ch for each st work 12dc over ch, *1dc into next 1ch sp on first round, ch7, turn.
2nd row 1dc into 7th dc of previous row, (ch1, skip 1dc, 1dc into next dc) 3 times, ch4, turn.
3rd row (1dc into next 1ch sp, ch1) 3 times, 13dc into 7ch loop.
Rep from * 10 times more.
Sl st into 3rd of first 13ch, turn, sl st across each of first 7dc of previous row, ch3, sl st into base of turning ch at outer edge of first row, (ch1, skip 1dc, 1dc into next dc) 3 times, ch4, turn, (1dc into next 1ch sp, ch1) 3 times, sl st into top of turning ch at outer edge of first row.
Fasten off.

Second motif
Work as given for First motif to end of first row.
2nd row 1dc into 7th dc of previous

row, (ch1, skip 1dc, 1dc into next dc) 3 times, ch3, sl st into corresponding 4ch at outer edge of any row of First motif, ch1, complete row as before.
Join the following row of the Second motif to the corresponding row of the First motif in the same way, then complete the second motif as given for the First motif.
Make a row of five motifs in all.
Make a second row of six motifs, joining each one to the motifs on either side in the same row and to the adjacent motifs in the first row.
Increase one motif in every row until there are nine and then decrease until there are five — 61 motifs in all, joined to form a hexagon as shown in the photograph.

Edging
With RS facing, rejoin yarn at 4ch loop on outer edge of the first free row on any motif, 5sc into 4ch loop, *ch7, 5sc into next free 4ch loop, rep from * all around, ending with 7ch, sl st into first sc.
2nd round Ch3, *13 dc into next 7ch loop, rep from * all around, ending with 12dc into last 7ch loop, sl st into 3rd of 3ch.
3rd round Ch 4, *skip first dc of next 13dc gr, (1dc into next dc, ch1, skip 1dc) 6 times, rep from * into each 13dc gr all around except when the 13dc gr links two motifs work instead skip 2dc, (1dc into next dc, ch1, skip 1dc) 5 times, and ending with sl st into 3rd of first 4ch.
Fasten off.

To finish
Press under a damp cloth, using a warm iron.

Enlarged detail showing the formation of the motif

Delicate oval place mats

Delicate oval place mats have centers made from three rounds surrounded by a distinctive oak leaf border and a fan edging.

Size
16½in long by 12¼in wide

Gauge
Each motif (see below) measures 1¾in in diameter worked on size 8 steel hook To save time, check your gauge.

Materials
Approx 531yds of a size 20 crochet cotton
Size 8 steel crochet hook

Note: See Working in fine cotton on page 14.

Place mat

First motif
Using size 8 steel hook, ch10, sl st into first ch to form a circle.
1st round Ch 3 to count as first dc, 23dc into circle. Join with a sl st to 3rd of first 3ch. 24dc.
2nd round 1sc into same place as sl st, *ch5, skip 1dc, 1sc into next dc, rep from * ending last rep with 2ch, 1dc into first sc. 12 loops.
3rd round 1sc into loop just made, *ch5, 1sc into next loop, rep from * ending last rep with 5ch, sl st into first sc.
4th round Sl st into each of next 3ch, ch3, 3dc into same place as last sl st, ch2, 4dc into center ch of next loop, rep from * ending last rep with 2ch, sl st into 3rd of first 3ch. Fasten off.

Second motif
Work first 3 rounds as for First motif.
4th round Sl st into each of next 3ch, ch3, 3dc into same place as last sl st, *ch1, sl st into corresponding sp on first motif, ch1, 4dc into center ch of next loop on Second motif, rep from *

once more, then complete as given for First motif.

Third motif
Work first 3 rounds as given for First motif. Join as Second motif was joined to first having 4 sps free on each side between joins. Do not fasten off.

Main section
1st round Sl st into next dc, ch2, 1dc into 3rd dc of first free group on next motif, *(ch5, 1sc into next sp, ch5, 1sc into 3rd dc of next group) 3 times, ch5, 1sc into next sp, ch5, leaving last loop of each st on hook work 1dc into 2nd dc of next group and 1dc into 3rd dc of first free group on next motif, yo and draw through all loops on hook — called 1 joint dc —, (ch5, 1sc into next sp, ch5, 1sc into 3rd dc of next group) 9 times, ch5, 1sc into next sp, ch5, 1 joint dc working 1dc into 2nd dc of next group and 1dc into 3rd dc of next group, rep from * omitting 5ch and join dc at end of last rep, ch2, 1dc into first dc. 56 loops.
2nd round Ch 2, 1dc into next loop, *(ch5, 1sc into next loop) 6 times, ch5, 1 joint dc over next 2 loops, (ch5, 1sc into next loop) 18 times, ch5, 1 joint dc over next 2 loops, rep from * omitting 5ch and joint dc at end of last rep, ch2, 1dc into first dc.
3rd round Ch 6, 1dc into last dc, *(into center ch of next loop work 1dc, 3ch and 1dc — called V st —) 13 times, (ch3, V st into center ch of next loop) 8 times, (V st into center ch of next loop) 5 times, rep from * omitting V st at end of last rep, sl st into 3rd of first 6ch.
4th round Sl st into first loop, ch6, 1dc into same loop, *(into sp of next V st work 1dc, ch3, 1dc — called V st over V st —) 13 times, (V st into next 3ch loop, V st into next sp of next V st)

8 times, (V st into sp of next V st) 5 times, rep from * omitting V st at end of last rep, sl st into 3rd of first 6ch.
5th round Sl st into first loop, ch6, 1dc into same loop, *4dc into sp of next V st, V st into sp of next V st, rep from * omitting V st at end of last rep, sl st into 3rd of first 6ch.
6th round Sl st into first loop, ch6, 1dc into same loop, *(skip 2dc of next group, V st into next dc, V st into sp of next V st) 7 times, (ch2, skip 2dc of next group, V st into next dc, ch2, V st into sp of next V st) 7 times, (skip 2dc of next group, V st into next dc, V st into sp of next V st) 3 times, rep from * omitting V st at end of last rep, sl st into 3rd of first 6ch.
7th round Sl st into first loop, ch6, 1dc into same loop, *(V st into sp of next V st) 14 times, (ch3, V st into sp of next V st) 14 times, (V st into sp of next V st) 6 times, rep from * omitting V st at end of last rep, sl st into 3rd of first 6ch.
8th round Sl st into each of first 5 sts and next sp, ch9, 1tr into same sp, *(ch3, skip 3dc, 1tr into next dc, ch3, skip next sp, into next sp work 1tr, ch5 and 1tr) 4 times, ch3, skip 2dc, 1tr into next dc, (ch3, skip next sp, into next sp work 1tr, 5ch and 1tr, ch3, skip next sp, 1tr into next sp) 6 times, ch3, skip next sp, into next sp work 1tr, 5ch and 1tr, ch3, skip 1dc, 1tr into next dc, ch3, skip next sp, into next sp work 1tr, 5ch, and 1tr, (ch3, skip 3dc, 1tr into next dc, ch3, skip next sp, into next sp work 1tr, 5ch and 1tr) twice, rep from * omitting 1tr, 5ch and 1tr at end of last rep, sl st into 4th of first 9ch.
9th round Sl st into first sp, ch9, 1tr into same sp, *ch3, skip 1tr, 1tr into next tr, ch3, skip next sp, into next sp work (1tr, 5ch and 1tr), rep from *

omitting 1tr, 5ch and 1tr at end of last rep, sl st into 4th of first 9ch.

10th round Sl st into first sp, ch4, into same sp work (3tr, 2ch, 1tr, 2ch and 4tr), *ch1, skip next sp, 1tr into next tr, ch1, into next 5ch sp work (4tr, 2ch, 1tr, 2ch, and 4tr), rep from * ending with ch1, skip next sp, 1tr into next tr, ch1, sl st into 4th of first 4ch.

11th round Ch 3, leaving last loop of each st on hook work 1tr into each of next 3tr, yo and draw through all loops on hook — called 3tr cluster —, *ch2, into next tr work (4tr, 2ch, 1tr, 2ch and 4tr), ch2, work 4tr cluster over next 4tr, ch1, 1tr into next tr, ch1, work 4tr cluster over next 4tr, rep from * omitting cluster at end of last rep. Join with a sl st to first cluster.

12th round Sl st into each of next 2ch and next tr, ch3, 3tr cluster over next 3tr, rep from * on previous round.

13th round As 12th.

14th round Sl st into each of first 2ch and next tr, ch3, 3tr cluster over next 3tr, * ch3, 4tr into next tr, ch3, 4tr cluster over next 4tr, ch2, into next tr work (1tr, 3ch and 1tr), ch2, 4tr cluster over next 4tr, rep from * omitting cluster at end of last rep. Join with a sl st to first cluster.

15th round Sl st into each of next 3ch and tr, ch3, 3tr cluster over next 3tr, *ch5, 1tr into next tr, ch3, into next loop work (1tr, 5ch and 1tr), ch3, 1tr into next tr, ch5, 4tr cluster over next 4tr, rep from * omitting 4tr cluster at end of last rep.
Join with a sl st to first cluster.

16th round 1sc into same place as last sl st, *ch3, (into next tr work 1tr, 3ch and 1tr) twice, into next loop work 1tr, 5ch and 1tr, (into next tr work 1tr, 3ch and 1tr) twice, ch3, 1sc into next cluster, rep from * omitting 1sc at end of last rep. Join with a sl st to first sc.

17th round 1sc into same place as last sl st, *ch5, skip next loop, 1tr into next loop, ch4, 1sc into 3rd ch from hook, ch1 — called picot —, 1tr into same loop, (into next loop work 1tr, picot, 1ch, 1tr and 1ch) 4 times, ch5, 1sc into next sc, rep from * omitting 1sc at end of last rep. Join with a sl st to first sc. Fasten off.

To finish

Dampen and pin out to correct shape, using stainless steel pins.
Leave to dry.

Lacy circular coasters

Make a mat and coasters in crisp, cream cotton to protect your furniture and, at the same time, to set off your most precious glasses.

Sizes
Large mat 9in diameter
Small mat 4in diameter

Gauge
First 3 rounds measure ¾in in diameter
To save time, check your gauge.

Materials
Approx 354yds of a size 20 crochet cotton
Size 8 steel crochet hook

Note: See Working in rounds on page 150 and Working in fine cotton on page 14.

Large mat
Ch20, sl st into first ch to form a circle.
1st round Ch3, 47dc into circle, sl st into 3rd of 3ch.
2nd round Ch5, (skip next dc, 1dc into next dc, ch2) 23 times, skip last dc, sl st into 3rd of 5ch.
3rd round Ch 6, (1dc into next dc, 3ch) to end, sl st into 3rd of 6ch.
4th round Ch 7, (1dc into next dc, ch4) to end, sl st into 3rd of 7ch.
5th round Ch 3, (4dc into next sp, 1dc into next dc) to end, sl st into 3rd of 3ch.
6th round 1sc into same place as sl st, 1sc into each of next 3dc, (15ch, skip next 8dc, 1sc into each of next 7dc) 8 times, omitting 4sc at end of last rep, sl st into first sc.
7th round 1sc into same place as sl st, *into next loop work (8dc, 5ch) twice and 8dc, skip next 3sc, 1sc into next sc, rep from * omitting 1sc at end of last rep, sl st into first sc.
8th round Sl st into each of next 10 sts, *1sc into next loop, ch7, 1sc into next loop, ch15, rep from * to end, sl st into first sc.

9th round Sl st into next st, ch4, *skip next st, 1dc into next st, ch1, rep from * to end, sl st into 3rd of 4ch.

10th – 13th rounds Ch 5, *1dc into next dc, ch2, rep from * to end, sl st into 3rd of 5ch.

14th – 16th rounds As 3rd round.

17th round Sl st into next sp, ch3, 2dc into same sp, 3dc into each sp, sl st into 3rd of 3ch.

18th round 1sc into same place as sl st, 1sc into each of next 4dc, *ch17, skip next 9dc, 1sc into each of next 9dc, rep from * omitting 5sc at end of last rep, sl st into first sc.

19th round 1sc into same place as sl st, 1sc into next sc, *into next loop work (9dc, 5ch) twice and 9dc, skip next 3sc, 1sc into each of next 3sc, rep from * omitting 2sc at end of last rep, sl st into first sc. Fasten off.

Small mat

Work as large mat to end of 7th round. Fasten off. Dampen, pin to correct measurements and let dry.

Alternatives

Enlarge our coasters to make place mats or change the pattern and make a hot pad or even a floor mat.

Our coasters are worked with a fine steel hook in a thin cotton yarn chosen for its crisp feel. But do not limit yourself to cotton when making circular shapes. Most circles can be made in thicker yarns like sport or knitting worsted. You can also use string or even rope to make solid circles for heatproof table mats or for floor mats. Some of the alternative circles can be worked to any size by continuing to work in rounds. To enlarge more elaborate patterns, try working them in a fairly thick yarn or with a larger hook. You can also make circles larger by working plain double crochet, double crochet and chain, or chain loops around the edges as we did in the place mat and coasters on page 64. Increase on every or every other round, checking as you go that the mat lies flat. To join a number of circles together to form a large mat, place them on a flat surface with right sides up and catchstitch each to its neighbors using a matching yarn.

More experienced crocheters may like to join rounds with picot mesh as in traditional Irish crochet.

Some of the alternative patterns are given in chart form using symbols. Symbols and charts are explained in Understanding crochet patterns on pages 11 – 13.

To begin a circle, either work the number of chains shown in the center of the chart or use the method described in Working a closed center on page 150. Work the rounds (as denoted by blue numbers) in counter-clockwise direction and join with a slip stitch (denoted by a heavy black chain).

Circular patterns

1 Spiral

This circle can be worked to any size. Use 2 colors, A and B.

Using A and leaving a long end, wind yarn twice around index finger to form a circle. Holding circle together, begin work:

1st round Ch 1, 5sc into circle, join with a sl st to first ch. If necessary, pull long end slightly to tighten circle.

2nd round Ch 1 in B, 1sc in B into same place as first ch, *(1sc in A, 1sc in B) into next st, rep from * to end, join with a sl st in A to first ch. From now on, work into back loop only of each st on every round.

3rd round Ch 1 in B, *2sc in B into next st, 1sc in A into next sc, rep from * to last st, 2sc in B into next st, join with a sl st in A to first ch.

4th round Ch 1 in B, *2sc in B into next sc, 1sc in A into each of next 2sc, rep from * to last 2 sts, 2sc in B into next st, 1sc in A into next st, join with a sl st in A to first ch.

5th round Ch 1 in B, *2sc in B into next sc, 1sc in A into each of next 3sc, rep from * to last 3 sts, 2sc in B into next sc, 1sc in A into each of next 2 sts, sl st in A to first ch.

Cont in this way on foll rounds, working 2sc into first sc of arms of spiral worked in B, and working one more sc in A between arms of spiral.

2 Wagon wheel

This circle can be worked to any size. Use 2 colors, A and B

Work as for basic circle (see Pattern 3). Begin and work first round in A, then work 2dc into 1dc alternately in A and B. Cont 3rd round as follows:

Ch3 in A, *using A, 1dc into next dc, 2dc into next dc, 1dc into next dc, using B, 2dc into next dc, rep from * to last st, using B, 1dc into last st, using A 1dc into base of 3ch, join with a sl st in A to 3rd of first 3ch.

Cont as given for basic circle, working 2dc into 2nd st worked in A on each spoke of wheel.

1

2

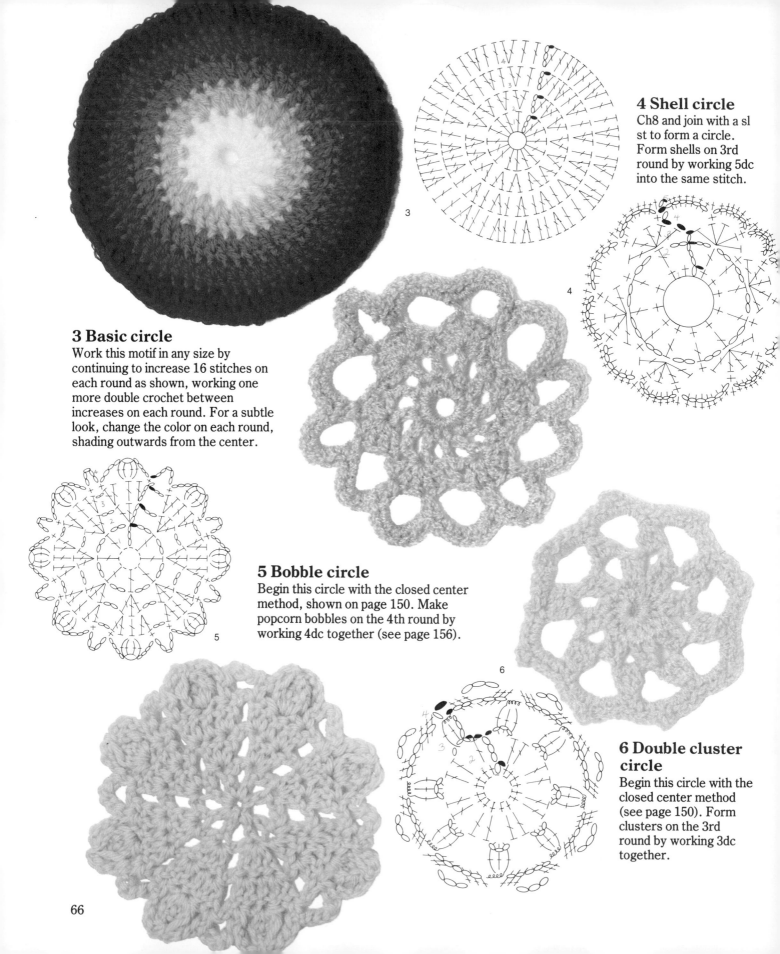

3 Basic circle

Work this motif in any size by continuing to increase 16 stitches on each round as shown, working one more double crochet between increases on each round. For a subtle look, change the color on each round, shading outwards from the center.

4 Shell circle

Ch8 and join with a sl st to form a circle. Form shells on 3rd round by working 5dc into the same stitch.

5 Bobble circle

Begin this circle with the closed center method, shown on page 150. Make popcorn bobbles on the 4th round by working 4dc together (see page 156).

6 Double cluster circle

Begin this circle with the closed center method (see page 150). Form clusters on the 3rd round by working 3dc together.

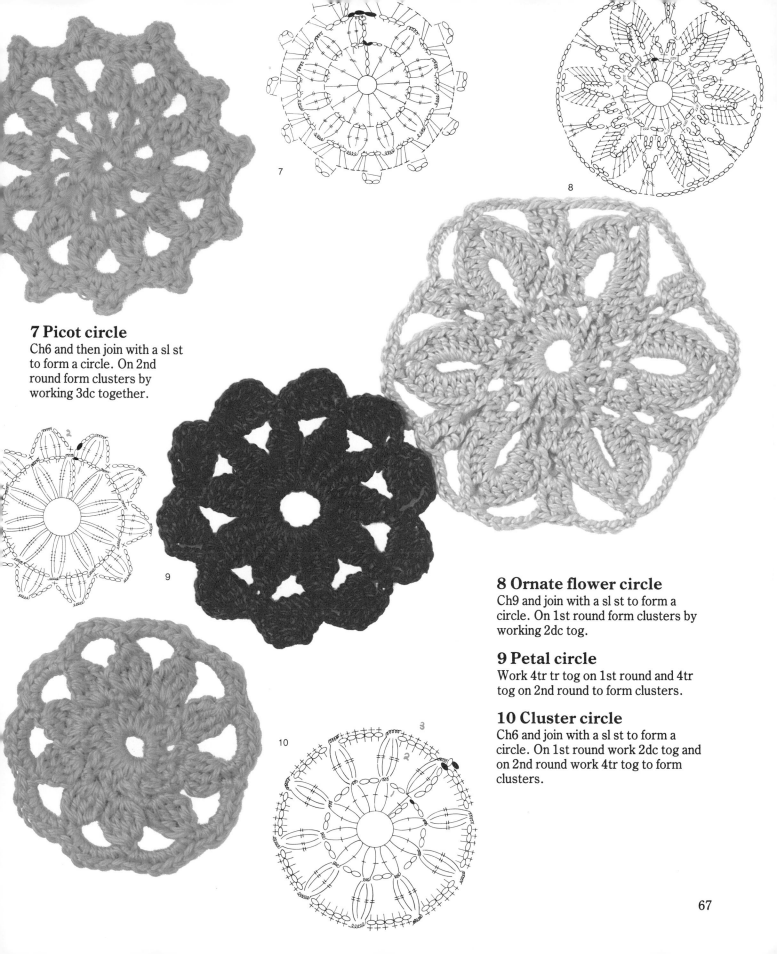

7 Picot circle

Ch6 and then join with a sl st
to form a circle. On 2nd
round form clusters by
working 3dc together.

8 Ornate flower circle

Ch9 and join with a sl st to form a
circle. On 1st round form clusters by
working 2dc tog.

9 Petal circle

Work 4tr tr tog on 1st round and 4tr
tog on 2nd round to form clusters.

10 Cluster circle

Ch6 and join with a sl st to form a
circle. On 1st round work 2dc tog and
on 2nd round work 4tr tog to form
clusters.

67

Star-struck tablecloth

A fine lacy tablecloth which can be made to any size.

Size

Large star shape measures 4¼in between widest points

Gauge

Small filling shape measures 1¼in between widest points
To save time, check your gauge.

Materials

Approx 177yds of a size 20 crochet cotton make 6 large stars and 6 small filling shapes
Size 8 steel crochet hook

Note: See Working an open center on page 150 and Working in fine cotton on page 14.

First star

**Using size 8 steel hook, wind yarn 20 times around tip of little finger to form a circle, sl st into circle.
1st round Ch 4, 3tr into circle, (ch3, 4tr into circle) 7 times, ch3, sl st to top of first 4ch.
2nd round Ch 1, 1sc into next tr, ch3, sl st to last sc worked — picot formed —, 1sc into each of next 2tr, *(1sc, ch3, 1sc) into next 3ch sp, 1sc into each of next 2tr, picot, 1sc into each of next 2tr, rep from * 7 times more, (1sc, ch3, 1sc) into next 3ch sp, sl st to first ch.
3rd round Sl st across first 4sc and into first 3ch sp, ch4, 1tr into same 3ch sp, (ch10, work 2tr tog into next 3ch sp) 7 times, ch10, sl st to top of first 4ch.
4th round Ch 1, (13sc into next 10ch sp) 8 times, sl st to first ch.
5th round Ch 4, skip next sc, (1dc into next sc, ch1, skip next sc) 51 times, sl st to 3rd of first 4ch.
6th round Ch 1, (2sc into next 1ch sp) 52 times, sl st to first ch.
7th round Sl st across first 4sc, (ch7, skip next 4sc, 1sc into next sc, ch10, skip next 7sc, 1sc into next sc) 8 times.**
8th round *(4sc, picot, 4sc) into next 7ch loop, 9sc into next 10ch loop, ch7, sl st into 5th of 9sc just worked, (4sc, picot, 4sc) into next 7ch loop, 4sc into remainder of 10ch loop, rep from * ending with sl st to first sc. Fasten off.

Second star

Work from ** to ** of First star.
8th round (4sc, picot, 4sc) into next 7ch loop, 9sc into next 10ch loop, ch7, sl st into 5th sc of 9sc just worked, (4sc, ch1, sl st to corresponding picot on First star, ch1, 4sc) into next 7ch loop, 4sc into remainder of 10ch loop, complete round as for 8th round of First star.
Continue working Second stars in this way until tablecloth is required width.

First filling shape

Begin and work 1st round as for First star.
2nd round Ch 1, 1sc into next tr, picot, 1sc into each of next 2tr, 1sc into next 3ch sp, ch1, sl st to large picot on inner edge of First star, ch1, 1sc into same 3ch sp, 1sc into each of next 2tr, picot, 1sc into each of next 2tr, (1sc, ch3, 1sc) into next 3ch sp, 1sc into each of next 2tr, picot, 1sc into each of next 2tr, 1sc into next 3ch sp, ch1, sl st to large picot on inner edge of Second star, complete round as for 2nd round of First star. Fasten off.
Continue working Filling shapes in the same way between large star motifs.

Next star row

Work from ** to ** as for First star.
8th round * (ch4, picot, ch4) into next 7ch loop, 9sc into next 10ch loop, ch7, sl st into 5th of 9sc just worked, (4sc, ch1, sl st to corresponding large picot on first star of previous Star row, ch1, 4sc) into next 7ch loop, 4sc into remainder of 10ch loop*, rep from * to * once, joining 1ch to corresponding 1ch sp on next Filling shape, complete round as for 8th round of First star.
Work foll large stars in the same way, joining each star to previous large star of this row, filling shape of previous row, next large star of previous row and next filling shape of previous row. Cont in this way until the tablecloth is required length, omitting filling shapes from last row of large stars.

Edging

With RS facing and using size 8 steel hook, join yarn to first picot of corner star.

1st round Ch 4, 1tr into same picot, ch10, 1sc into next large picot, (ch10, 1sc into next picot, ch10, 1sc into next large picot) 4 times, ch10, work 2tr tog into last picot of same star, *work 2tr tog into first picot of next star, (ch10, 1sc into next large picot, ch10, 1sc into next picot) 3 times omitting 1sc at end of last rep, work 2tr tog into last large picot, rep from * to end, working extra 10ch loops on corner stars as required, sl st to top of first 4ch.
2nd round (7sc, picot, 7sc) into first loop, *9sc into next loop, ch7, sl st into 5th of 9sc just worked, (4sc, picot, 4sc) into next 7ch loop, 4sc into remainder of 10ch loop*, rep, from * to * 7 times more, **(7sc, picot, 7sc) into next loop**, rep from ** to ** once more, rep from * to * 4 times more, cont in this way, working extra picot points at each corner as required, sl st to first sc. Fasten off.

To finish

Darn in all ends.
Press tablecloth under a damp cloth.

Alternatives

Make a heavenly tablecloth using delicate crochet stars.

Like squares, hexagons and circles, stars can be made separately and joined together to make a fabric. But because they have sharp points, they leave large holes between them which are usually filled with smaller shapes to make a delicate lace fabric. To vary the effect, you can change the color — try white over a red cloth for Christmas, for example. Or use two colors. The filling shapes could be done in a lighter shade of the color of the stars or in a contrasting color.
Another way to vary the tablecloth is to use a different star pattern altogether.
Stars are best worked in a smooth, crisp yarn so they will retain their shape. Cotton is ideal, but synthetic yarns of the same texture are also suitable. The thickness of the yarn determines the size of the star — the thicker the yarn, the larger the star.

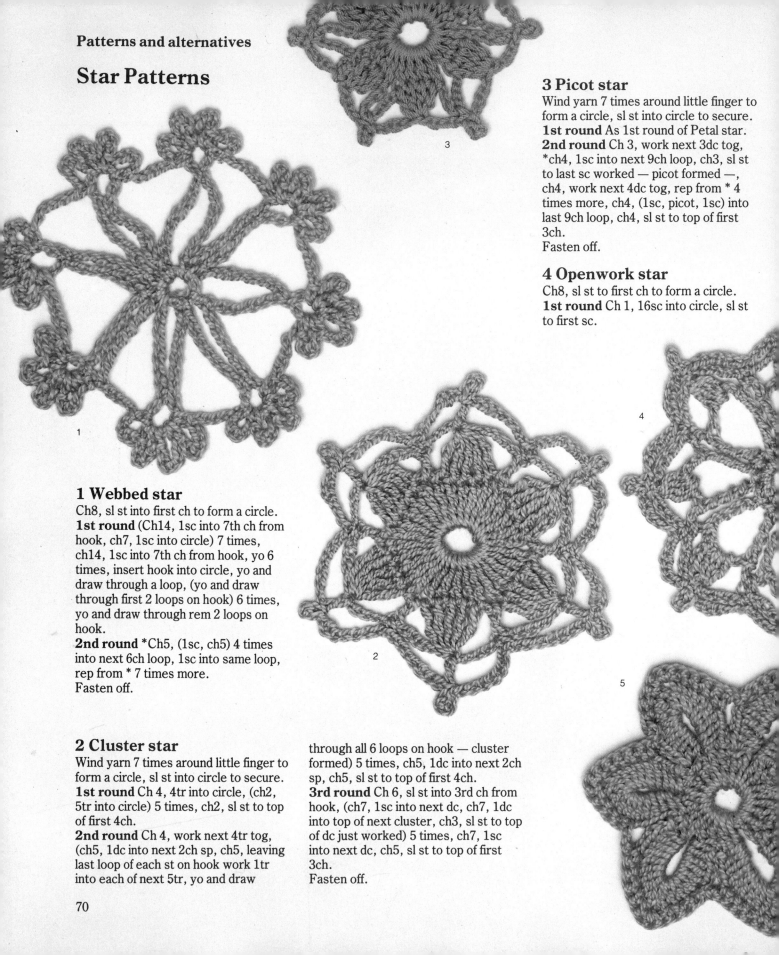

Star Patterns

3 Picot star

Wind yarn 7 times around little finger to form a circle, sl st into circle to secure.
1st round As 1st round of Petal star.
2nd round Ch 3, work next 3dc tog, *ch4, 1sc into next 9ch loop, ch3, sl st to last sc worked — picot formed —, ch4, work next 4dc tog, rep from * 4 times more, ch4, (1sc, picot, 1sc) into last 9ch loop, ch4, sl st to top of first 3ch.
Fasten off.

4 Openwork star

Ch8, sl st to first ch to form a circle.
1st round Ch 1, 16sc into circle, sl st to first sc.

1 Webbed star

Ch8, sl st into first ch to form a circle.
1st round (Ch14, 1sc into 7th ch from hook, ch7, 1sc into circle) 7 times, ch14, 1sc into 7th ch from hook, yo 6 times, insert hook into circle, yo and draw through a loop, (yo and draw through first 2 loops on hook) 6 times, yo and draw through rem 2 loops on hook.
2nd round *Ch5, (1sc, ch5) 4 times into next 6ch loop, 1sc into same loop, rep from * 7 times more.
Fasten off.

2 Cluster star

Wind yarn 7 times around little finger to form a circle, sl st into circle to secure.
1st round Ch 4, 4tr into circle, (ch2, 5tr into circle) 5 times, ch2, sl st to top of first 4ch.
2nd round Ch 4, work next 4tr tog, (ch5, 1dc into next 2ch sp, ch5, leaving last loop of each st on hook work 1tr into each of next 5tr, yo and draw

through all 6 loops on hook — cluster formed) 5 times, ch5, 1dc into next 2ch sp, ch5, sl st to top of first 4ch.
3rd round Ch 6, sl st into 3rd ch from hook, (ch7, 1sc into next dc, ch7, 1dc into top of next cluster, ch3, sl st to top of dc just worked) 5 times, ch7, 1sc into next dc, ch5, sl st to top of first 3ch.
Fasten off.

2nd round Ch 11, 1dtr into next sc, (ch3, 1dtr into next sc, ch6, 1dtr into next sc) 7 times, ch3, sl st to 5th of first 11ch.
3rd round Sl st into each of first 2ch, ch3, work 3dc tog into same 6ch loop of previous round, (ch5, 1sc into next 3ch loop, ch5, work 4dc tog into next 6ch loop) 7 times, ch5, 1sc into next 3ch loop, ch5, 1sc into top of first 3ch.
4th round (ch3, sl st to last sc worked — picot formed —, ch6, 1sc into next sc, ch6, 1sc into top of next cluster) 8 times, omitting last sc and ending with sl st to beg of round.
Fasten off.

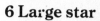

6 Large star
Ch10, sl st to first ch to form a circle.
1st round Ch 4, 3tr into circle, (ch3, 4tr into circle) 7 times, ch3, sl st to top of first 4ch.
2nd round Ch 4, work next 3tr tog, (ch6, 1sc into next 3ch loop, ch6, work next 4tr tog) 7 times, ch6, 1sc into next 3ch loop, ch6, sl st to top of first 4ch.
3rd round 8sc into first 6ch loop, *8sc into next 6ch loop, 4sc into next 6ch loop, ch5, sl st into 4th of 8sc just worked, (4sc, ch3, sl st to last sc worked — picot formed —, 4sc) into next 5ch loop, 4sc into rem of 6ch loop, rep from * 6 times more, 8 sc into next 6ch loop, sl st into each of next 4sc, ch5, sl st into 4th sc just worked, (4sc, picot, 4sc) into next 5ch loop, sl st to next sc.
Fasten off.

7 Chain star
Wind yarn 7 times around little finger to form a circle, sl st into circle to secure.
1st round Ch 3, 2dc into circle, (ch9, 3dc into circle) 7 times, ch9, sl st into top of first 3ch.
2nd round (1sc into next dc, ch4, 1sc into next 9ch loop, ch4, skip next dc) 8 times.
3rd round (1sc into next sc, ch5, 1sc into next 4ch loop, ch3, sl st to last sc worked — picot formed —, 1sc into next 4ch loop, ch5) 8 times, sl st to first sc.
Fasten off.

8 Petal star
Wind yarn 7 times around little finger to form a circle, sl st into circle to secure.
1st round Ch 3, 3dc into circle, (ch9, 4dc into circle) 5 times, ch9, sl st to top of first 3ch.
2nd round *Ch3, 9sc into next 9ch loop, ch5, sl st into 5th sc worked, 7sc into 5ch loop just worked, 4sc into same 9ch loop, rep from * to end.
Fasten off.

5 Triple star
Wind yarn 7 times around little finger to form a circle, sl st into circle to secure.
1st round As 1st round of Petal star.
2nd round Sl st into first dc, *1sc into next dc, (9dc, ch2, 9dc) into next 9ch loop, skip next 2dc, rep from * 5 times more, sl st into first sc. Turn.
3rd round Sl st into each of first 4dc, *1sc into each of next 5dc, 2sc into next 2ch loop, 1sc into each of next 5dc, ch2, skip next 8dc, rep from * 5 times more, sl st to first sc.
Fasten off.

71

Webbed sideboard runner

A webbed runner will decorate the top of your sideboard or dresser and protect its highly polished surface.

Size
15in × 60in

Gauge
28dc and 15 rows over dc pat on size 0 steel crochet hook
To save time, check your gauge.

Materials
Approx 1500yds of a size 6 crochet cotton
Size 0 steel crochet hook

Note: See Working an approximate foundation on page 152.

Runner
Ch103.
Base row 1dc into 4th ch from hook, 1dc into each ch to end. Turn. 101dc.
1st row Ch 3, skip first st, *1dc into each of next 2dc, ch5, (skip next 2dc, 1tr into next dc) 3 times, ch5, skip next 2dc, 1dc into next dc, rep from * to last 2 sts, 1dc into each of last 2 sts. Turn.
2nd row Ch 3, skip first st, *1dc into each of next 2dc, ch4, skip next 4ch, 1sc into next ch, 1sc into each of next 3tr, 1sc into next ch, ch4, skip next 4ch, 1dc into next dc, rep from * to last 2 sts, 1dc into each of last 2 sts. Turn.
3rd row Ch 3, skip first st, *1dc into each of next 2dc, ch5, skip next sc, 1sc into each of next 3sc, ch5, skip next sc, 1dc into next dc, rep from * to last 2 sts, 1dc into each of last 2 sts. Turn.
4th row Ch 3, skip first st, *1dc into each of next 2dc, (ch2, 1tr into next sc) 3 times, ch2, 1dc into next dc, rep from * to last 2 sts, 1dc into each of last 2 sts. Turn.
5th row Ch 3, skip first st, *1dc into each of next 2dc, (2dc into next 2ch sp, 1dc into next tr) 3 times, 2dc into next 2ch sp, 1dc into next dc, rep from * to last 2 sts, 1dc into each of last 2 sts. Turn.
1st – 5th rows form pat. Rep them until work measures approx 58in, ending with a 5th pat row.
Do not finish off but cont along side of work for edging.

Edging
1st round Ch 3, 2dc into top of last dc, 2dc inserting hook into side of same dc, *2dc into side of next dc, rep from * until next corner is reached. Work 3dc into ch at corner, 1dc into each foundation ch, 3dc into next corner, 2dc into side of each dc on remaining side edge, 3dc into top of dc at next corner, 1dc into each dc at top edge, sl st to top of 3ch at beg.
2nd round Ch 3, 1dc into each dc all around, working 3dc into each corner st, sl st to top of 3ch at beg.
3rd round As 2nd round. Fasten off.

To finish
Cover with a damp cloth and press with a warm iron.

Alternatives
Use fine cotton yarn to spin some of the pretty alternative webs below.

Webbed patterns get their name from their resemblance to spider's webs. Because most are made from lengths of chain caught together with single crochet stitches, they are easy to make and suitable for beginners. Start with a place mat and work up to a bedspread. Webbed patterns look best when worked in fine plain yarn. A tightly twisted cotton or synthetic in any thickness from size 3 to size 60 is best. An elaborate yarn would obscure the pattern and a thicker one would reduce the fine, spider-web effect. The alternative samples were made in size 5 pearl cotton. See Working in fine cotton on page 14.
The directions for our alternative patterns are given in symbols. These charts look complicated, but once you understand them, they are surprisingly easy to follow. If you are unfamiliar with symbols, see the section on symbols and charts under Understanding crochet patterns on pages 11 – 13.

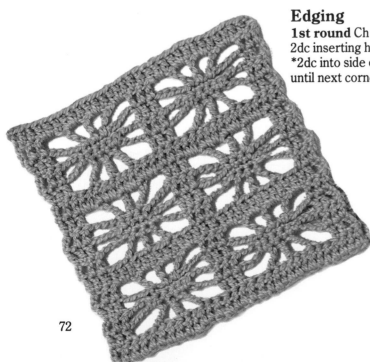

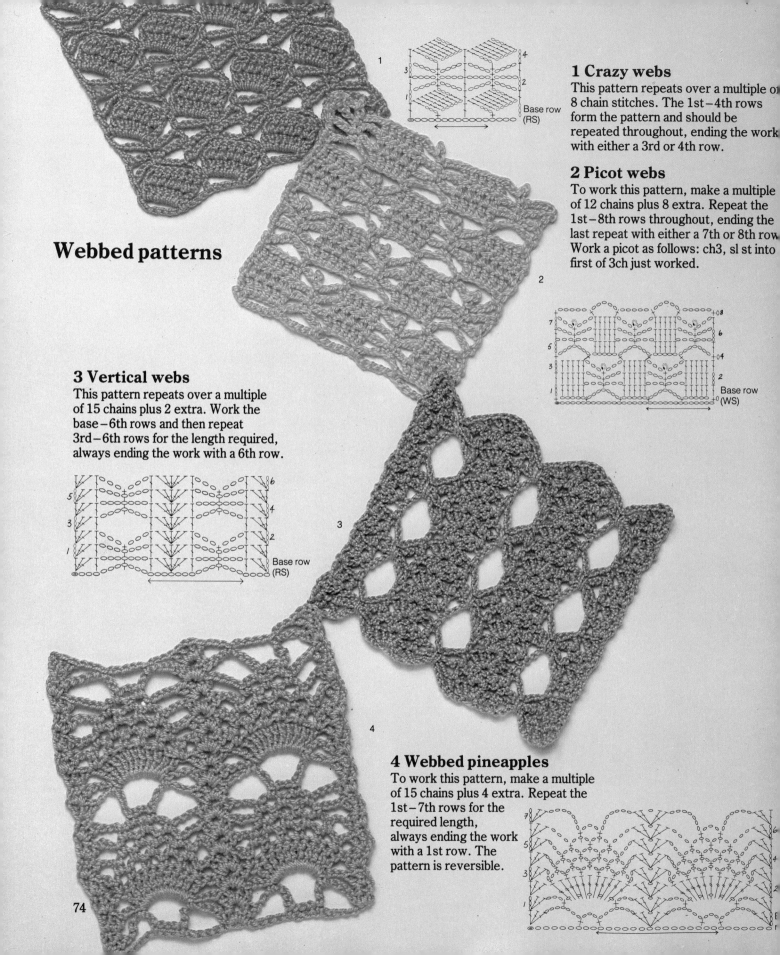

Webbed patterns

1 Crazy webs

This pattern repeats over a multiple of 8 chain stitches. The 1st–4th rows form the pattern and should be repeated throughout, ending the work with either a 3rd or 4th row.

2 Picot webs

To work this pattern, make a multiple of 12 chains plus 8 extra. Repeat the 1st–8th rows throughout, ending the last repeat with either a 7th or 8th row. Work a picot as follows: ch3, sl st into first of 3ch just worked.

3 Vertical webs

This pattern repeats over a multiple of 15 chains plus 2 extra. Work the base–6th rows and then repeat 3rd–6th rows for the length required, always ending the work with a 6th row.

4 Webbed pineapples

To work this pattern, make a multiple of 15 chains plus 4 extra. Repeat the 1st–7th rows for the required length, always ending the work with a 1st row. The pattern is reversible.

74

Curtains and rugs

Art nouveau filet curtain

The strong lines and flowing plant patterns of art nouveau design are captured forever in this filet crochet curtain.

Size
Approx 25in × 28¾in excluding edging

Gauge
20 sps and 20 rows to 4in over filet mesh worked on size 8 steel crochet hook
To save time, check your gauge.

Materials
Approx 1600yds of a size 20 crochet cotton
Size 8 steel crochet hook

Note: See Working in fine cotton on page 14, Filet crochet on page 161 and Lacets on page 157.

Curtain
Using size 8 steel hook ch384.
Base row (RS) 1dc into 4th ch from hook, 1dc into each of next 5ch, — 2 blocks or blks made —, * (ch2, skip next 2ch, 1dc into next ch) 3 times — 3 sps made —, 1dc into each of next 9ch — another 3 blks made —, rep from * 19 times more, (ch2, skip next 2ch, 1dc into next ch) 3 times, 1dc into each of next 6ch. Turn.
1st row Ch 5, skip first 3dc, 1dc into next dc — sp made over blk at beg of row —, 1dc into each of next 3dc, — blk made over blk —, 2dc into next sp, 1dc into next dc — blk made over sp —, (1sp, 2 blks, 1sp) 41 times. Turn.
2nd row Ch 3, work 126 blks, 2dc into next sp, 1dc into 3rd of last 5ch, (blk made over sp at end of row). Turn.
3rd row Ch 3, skip first dc, 1dc into each of next 3dc — blk made over blk at beg of row —, 1 blk, (3 sps, 3 blks) 20 times, 3 sps, 1 blk, 1dc into each of next 2dc, 1dc into 3rd of last 3ch — blk made over blk at end of row —. Turn.
4th – 16th rows Follow chart, always working from left to right until the

center is reached, then omitting the last blk or sp on the chart (as this is the central one) work back to the left for the 2nd half of the curtain, thus working the pattern in reverse.

17th row Work 5 sps, 15 blks, 3 sps, 2 blks, (ch3, skip next 2 sts, 1sc into next dc, ch3, skip next 2 sts, 1dc into next st) 3 times — 3 lacets made —, follow chart to end of row. Turn.

18th row Ch 5, 6 sps, 7 blks, 2 sps, 3 blks, 2 sps, 2 blks, ch5, skip next 5 sts, 1dc into next st — bar made —, (ch5, 1dc into next dc) 3 times — 3 bars made over 3 lacets —, 4 blks, follow chart to end of row. Turn.

19th row Ch 5, 14 sps, 3 blks, 2 sps, 1 blk, 3 lacets, 2 sps, 5dc over next bar, 1dc into next dc — 2 blks made over bar —, 2 sps, follow chart to end of row.

20th – 46th rows Follow chart.

47th row 17 sps, 2 blks, 1 sp, 1 blk, 2 sps, 2dc over next bar, 1dc into center ch of same bar, ch2, 1dc into next dc — blk and sp made over bar —, 1 sp, follow chart to end of row. Work 48th–155th rows from chart. Fasten off.

Edging

Using size 8 steel hook rejoin yarn to the botton right-hand corner, 1sc into same place as join, *2sc into next row-end, 1sc into next st*, rep from * to * along side edge working last sc into 3rd of 5ch at corner, 24ch, sl st into last sc (— a loop made —), (2sc into next sp, 1sc into next dc, 24ch, sl st into last sc) 127 times, rep from * to * along next side working last sc into foundation ch at corner, 2sc into same place as last sc, 1sc into each of next 6 sts, ch8, count back over the last 8sc just worked, sl st into next sc, working into the 8ch loop just made work (3sc, ch3) 3 times and 3sc, sl st into the last of the 6sc worked just before the 8ch — a scallop made —, 2sc into next sp, 1sc into next st, (1sc, ch3, and 1sc) into next sp, 1sc into next st, 2sc into next sp, (1sc into each of next 10 sts, ch8, count back over the last 9sc just worked and complete scallop as before, 2sc into next sp, 1sc into next st, (1sc, ch3, and 1sc) into next sp, 1sc into next st, 2sc into next sp) 20 times, 1sc into each of next 6 sts, 2sc into same place as first sc, sl st into first sc, ch8, count back over the last 7sc just worked and complete scallop as before. Fasten off.

To finish

With rustproof pins, pin out the curtain to size, dampen and leave to dry. Do not press.

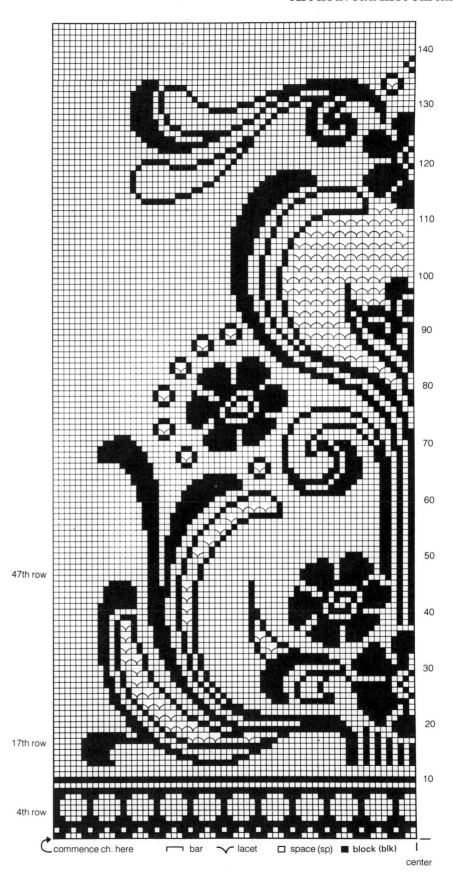

47th row

17th row

4th row

↻ commence ch. here   ⌐ bar   ⋎ lacet   ☐ space (sp)   ■ block (blk) |

center

140
130
120
110
100
90
80
70
60
50
40
30
20
10

Rag rug

This rug looks at home anywhere in the house. Choose colors to blend with the room.

Size
The rug measures approx 37in in diameter

Gauge
First 4 rounds measure approx 3½in in diameter
To save time, check your gauge.

Materials
Approx 22yds of cotton or cotton-polyester in assorted patterns
Size K crochet hook

Note: Quantity of fabric depends on weight of fabric and width of strips, and is therefore only approximate.

Note: To avoid a "stepped" appearance, introduce new fabric as follows. After working last sc in old fabric, insert hook into first sc of round and draw through new fabric. Using new fabric, 1sc into same place as join and cont in pat.

To make
Cut bias strips approx 1¼in wide from fabric. Join strips with machine stitching (see Fabric work on page 164) and wind into balls.
Using size K hook and fabric strip, ch6, sl st into first ch to form a circle.
1st round 12sc into circle. Do not join this or any foll round with a sl st. (See Working continuous rounds on page 151)
2nd round (1sc into next sc, 2sc into next sc) to end. 18sc.
3rd round (1sc into each of next 2sc, 2sc into next sc) to end. 24sc.
4th and every foll alt round 1sc into each sc to end.
5th round (1sc into each of next 3sc, 2sc into next sc) to end. 30sc.
7th round (1sc into each of next 4sc, 2sc into next sc) to end. 36sc. Cont to

inc 6sc in this way on 9th and every foll alt round until 24 rounds have been worked. 84sc.
25th round (1sc into each of next 6sc, 2sc into next sc) to end. 96sc.
26th round (1sc into each of next 7sc, 2sc into next sc) to end. 108sc. Cont to inc 12sc in this way on 29th and every foll alt round until rug measures approx 37in in diameter.
Next round 1sc into each sc to end.
Next round 1sc into each sc to end, join with a sl st to first sc. Fasten off.

Alternatives

The possibilities are endless when you crochet with fabric.

Most types of fabric can be used to crochet — we used nylon net, lurex, satin, cotton and pure wool in the following samples to give you an idea of the range.
Choose the fabric according to the type of article you are making. Lightweight cotton would be appropriate for a bag to hold crochet projects or place mats, for example. Heavier fabrics such as wool can be used for a hall rug.
Before you make a rug, decide where you will be using it. Lightweight and novelty fabrics may be acceptable for bedrooms, but kitchens need rugs made in heavier fabrics. In addition, remember that although bias strips are less likely to fray, fabrics that fray heavily should not be used for articles that require frequent laundering.

Estimating quantities
It is not easy to calculate the amount of fabric you will need when working fabric crochet. The best method is to work one row with the strip and then undo it. By measuring the length of strip required to work one row, you should be able to estimate roughly the amount needed to work the entire article.

Appearance
Working a row of crochet or working the gauge sample will help you get some idea of what kind of pattern the fabric will produce, but the final appearance of fabric work is not always predictable.
There are, however, some general guide lines. Solid fabrics will of course produce solid-colored crochet. Small prints will look like a solid version of the dominant color. Stripes and large prints look random-dyed when they are crocheted.

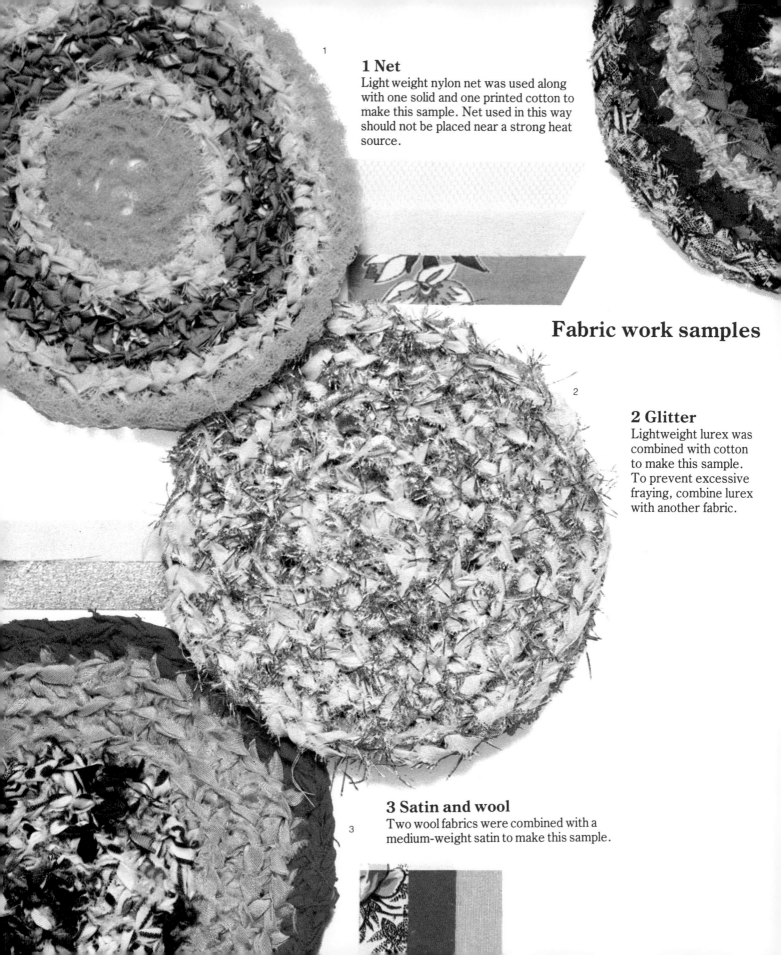

Fabric work samples

1 Net
Light weight nylon net was used along with one solid and one printed cotton to make this sample. Net used in this way should not be placed near a strong heat source.

2 Glitter
Lightweight lurex was combined with cotton to make this sample. To prevent excessive fraying, combine lurex with another fabric.

3 Satin and wool
Two wool fabrics were combined with a medium-weight satin to make this sample.

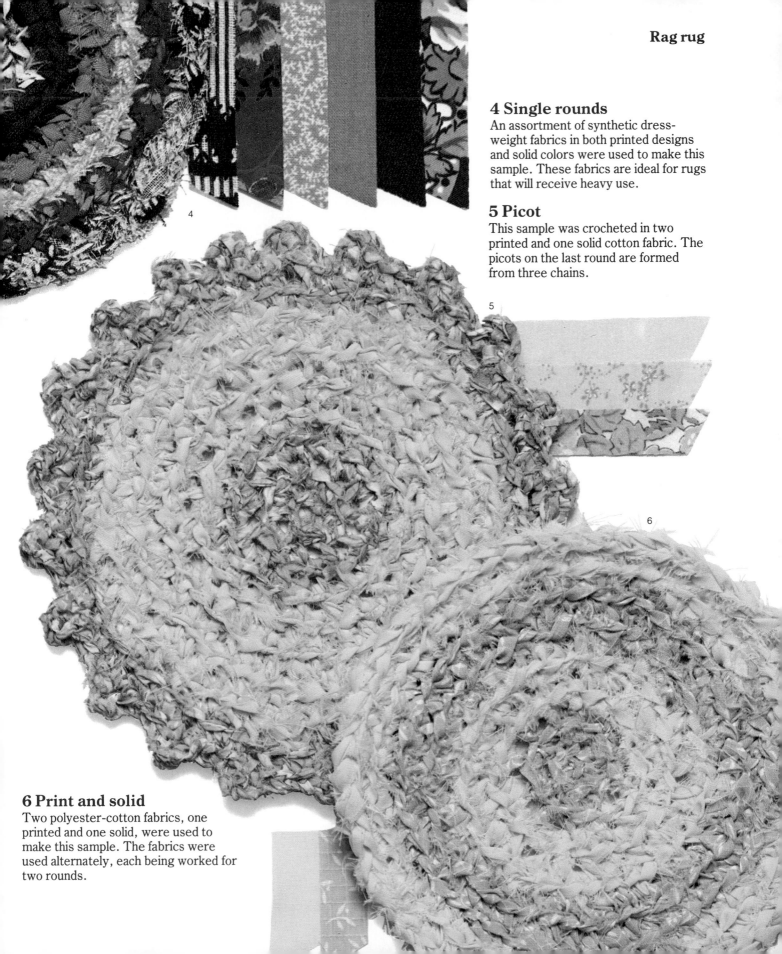

4 Single rounds

An assortment of synthetic dress-weight fabrics in both printed designs and solid colors were used to make this sample. These fabrics are ideal for rugs that will receive heavy use.

5 Picot

This sample was crocheted in two printed and one solid cotton fabric. The picots on the last round are formed from three chains.

6 Print and solid

Two polyester-cotton fabrics, one printed and one solid, were used to make this sample. The fabrics were used alternately, each being worked for two rounds.

Abstract design filet curtain

A filet curtain designed to fit a particular window or door
and worked in a rich color gives privacy and casts a pleasant
light in a room. Work two or three rows of double crochet at
the top of the filet pattern to give a firm edge for hanging.

Size
Café curtain measures approx
18½in × 30in

Gauge
1 block or 1 space = ½in
To save time, check your gauge

Materials
Approx 6oz of a size 3 crochet cotton
Size B crochet hook
Brass curtain rod and split brass rings

Note: See Filet crochet on page 161.

To make
Ch 147.
1st row: 1 dc in 4th ch from hook, 1dc
in each of next 2ch, * (ch2, skip 2ch,
1dc in each of next 4ch) twice, (ch2,
skip 2ch, 1dc in next ch) twice, 1dc in
each of next 6ch, (ch2, skip 2ch, 1dc in
next ch) 3 times, 1dc in each of next
3ch, (ch2, skip 2ch, 1dc in next ch) 4
times, 1dc in each of next 3ch,* (ch2,
skip 2ch, 1dc in each of next 4ch)
twice, (ch2, skip 2ch, 1dc in next ch) 3
times, 1dc in each of next 6ch, (ch2,
skip 2ch, 1dc in next ch) twice, 1dc in
each of next 6ch, rep from * to .*

Cont in pat from chart until work
measures 30in from beg, or length
required.
Next row: Ch3, 1dc in each dc and 2dc
in each sp to end.
Next row: Ch3, 1dc in each dc to end.
Repeat the last row once. Fasten off.
To hang, slide hooks between double
crochet stitches at top edge.

Child's "sheepskin" rug

Here's a rug to delight any child — a warm and woolly sheep standing in lush green grass. It would make a super Christmas or birthday gift.

Gauge

12 sts and 14 rows to 4in worked over sc loops

12 sts and 14 rows to 4in worked over hdc loops

To save time, check your gauge.

Materials

Knitting worsted or double knitting

53oz in (A)

15oz in (B)

2oz in (C)

Size H crochet hook

Note: See Working loop stitches on page 158.

Grass and legs section

Using size H crochet hook and B ch124.

Base row Work 1sc into the 2nd ch from hook, 1sc into each ch to end. Turn. 123sc.

1st row (WS) Ch1, to form a firm edge work into the first and last st throughout, *make a loop into the next st winding the yarn once around two fingers, rep from *working one loop into each st to end of row. Turn. 123 loops.

2nd row Ch 1, 1sc into each st to end. Turn. 123sc.

These 2 rows form the pat. Rep them 3 times more, then work the 1st row again.

Divide one ball of C into four small balls for legs.

10th row Ch 1, with B work 1sc into each of next 30 sts, joining first ball of C on last sc, with C work 1sc into each of next 6sc rejoining B on last st, with B work 1sc into each of next 42sc, join 2nd ball of C, with C work 1sc into each of next 6sc, joining B on last st, with B work 1sc into each of next 39sc. Turn.

11th – 13th rows Twisting yarns when changing color to avoid a hole, cont in loop pat for grass and sc for legs, as before.

14th row Ch 1, working in sc work 30B, 6C, 3B joining third ball of C on last sc, 6C, 33B, 6C, 3B joining fourth ball of C on last sc, 6C, 30B. Turn.

15th – 27th rows Work in pat as set, ending with a WS loop row. Fasten off 1st and 2nd balls of C.

28th row Ch 1, work 24sc, turn.

29th – 31st rows Work in pat on these 24sc as before.

32nd row Ch 1, work 18sc, turn.

33rd – 34th rows Work in pat on these 18sc as set.

35th row Sl st over first 3 sts, ch1, work a loop st into each of next 15 sts, turn.

36th – 38th rows Work in pat on these 15 sts as set.

39th row Sl st over first 6 sts, ch1, work a loop st into each of next 9 sts, turn.

40th and 41st rows Work in pat on these 9 sts as before. Fasten off.

42nd row Return to the 3rd leg in C

35in

41in

and ch1, 1sc into first st, 1sc into each of next 5 sts, joining B on last st, with B work 1sc into each of next 30sc. Turn.

43rd – 45th rows Work in pat on sts as before, ending with a WS loop row. Fasten off C.

46th row Ch 1, 1sc into first st, 1sc into each of next 23 sts. Turn.

47th – 49th rows Work in pat on these 23 sts as before. Fasten off.

50th row Return to the 4th leg in C and ch1, 1sc into first st, 1sc into each of next 5 sts joining B on last st, with B work 1sc into each of next 30 sts. Turn.

51st – 53rd rows Work in pat as before, ending with a WS loop row. Fasten off C.

54th row Sl st over first 3 loop sts, ch1, work 1sc into first st, 1sc into each of next 26 sts. Turn.

55th and 56th rows Work in pat on these 27 sts, turn.

57th row Ch 1, work a loop st into each of next 24 sts, turn.

58th – 63rd rows Work in pat on these 24 sts, ending with a WS loop row. Fasten off.

Sheep body section

Using size H crochet hook and A ch32.

1st row (RS) Work 1hdc into 3rd chain from hook, 1hdc into each ch to end. Turn. 30hdc.

2nd row * Chain 8, work 1sc into the back loop only of next st, rep from * to end. Turn. 30ch loops.

Cont to work 1 row hdc and 1 row loop pat throughout, inc as foll:

3rd row Inc thus: ch6, sl st into 2nd ch from hook, sl st into each of the next 2ch, 1hdc into the first loop skipped on previous row, 1hdc into each st to end. Turn. 30hdc.

4th row Inc thus: Chain 14, 1sc into the back loop of the 9th ch from hook, work an 8 chain loop into each of the next 5 ch, *ch8, 1sc into back loop only of next st, rep from * to end working across slipped sts. Turn. 39 loops.

5th row Ch 2, 1hdc into each of next 39 sts, turn.

6th row * Ch 8, 1sc into back loop only of next st, rep from * to end. Turn. 39 loops.

7th row Inc as for 3rd row, then work 39hdc. Turn.

8th row Inc as for 4th row, then work loop pat to end. Turn. 48 loops.

9th row Ch 2, 1hdc into each of next 48 sts. Turn.

10th row Work to end. Turn. 48 loops.

11th row As 9th.

12th row As 10th.

13th row Inc as for 3rd row, work 48hdc. Turn.

14th row Ch 11, 1sc into the back loop of the 9th ch from hook, work an 8 chain loop into each of the next 2ch, work loop pat to end of row. Turn. 54 loops.

15th and 16th rows Work to end. Turn.

17th row Inc as for 3rd row, work to end. Turn.

18th row Inc as for 14th row, work to end. Turn. 60 loops.

19th – 23rd rows Work to end. Turn.

24th row Inc as for 14th row, work to end. Turn. 63 loops.

25th – 38th rows Work to end. Turn.

39th row Sl st into each of next 3 sts, ch2, work 1hdc into each of next 60 sts. Turn.

85

40th – 42nd rows Work to end. Turn. 60 loops.

43rd row Ch 2, 1hdc into each of next 57 sts, turn.

44th – 48th rows Work to end. Turn.

49th row Ch 2, sl st into each of next 3 sts, ch2, 1hdc into each of next 51 sts, turn.

50th – 76th rows Work to end. Turn.

77th row Inc as for 3rd row, work 51hdc, turn.

78th row Inc as for 14th row, work to end. Turn. 57 loops.

79th and 80th rows Work to end. Turn.

81st row Inc as for 3rd row, work 57hdc. Turn.

82nd and 83rd rows Work to end. Turn.

84th row Inc as for 14th row. Work to end. Turn. 63 loops.

85th row Inc as for 3rd row, work 63hdc. Turn.

86th – 88th rows Work to end. Turn. 66 sts.

89th row Inc as for 3rd row. Work to end. Turn.

90th – 94th rows Work in pat on these 69 sts. Turn.

95th row Inc as for 3rd row, work to end. Turn. 69hdc.

96th – 98th rows Work in pat on these 72 sts. Turn.

99th row Inc as for 3rd row, work 69hdc, turn.

100th – 102nd rows Work in pat on these 72 sts, turn.

103rd row Inc as for 3rd row, work to end. Turn.

104th – 108th rows Work in pat on

these 75 sts. Turn.

109th row Inc as for 3rd row, work 72hdc, turn.

110th row Work across first 54 sts, turn.

111th and 112th rows Work to end. Turn.

113th row Sl st over first 3 sts, ch2, work 1hdc into each of next 45 sts, turn.

114th – 116th rows Work in pat on these 45 sts. Turn.

117th row Sl st over first 3 sts, ch2, work 1hdc into each of next 39 sts, turn.

118th – 120th rows Work in pat on these 39 sts. Turn.

121 st row Sl st over first 3 sts, ch2, work 1hdc into each of next 27 sts, turn.

122nd row Work in pat on these 27 sts. Turn.

123rd row Ch 2, work 1hdc into each of next 24 sts, turn.

124th – 126th rows Work to end. Turn.

127th row Sl st over first 3 sts, ch2, work 1hdc into each of next 12 sts, turn.

128th – 130th rows Work in pat on these 12 sts.
Fasten off.

131st row With WS facing skip next 3 sts, rejoin A to next st, work a loop st into each of next 18 sts. Turn.

132nd and 133rd rows Work to end. Turn.

134th row Ch 2, 1hdc into each of next 15 sts, turn.

135th – 137th rows Work to end. Turn.

138th row Ch 2, work 1hdc into each of next 9 sts, turn.

139th – 142nd rows Work to end. Turn.

143rd row Inc as for 14th row, work to end. Turn. 12 loops.

144th row Work to end. Turn.

145th row Inc as for 14th row, work a loop st into each of next 12 sts. Turn.

146th row Sl st over first 3 sts, ch2, work 1hdc into each of next 12 sts. Turn.

147th – 149th rows Work to end. Turn.

150th row Sl st over first 3 sts, ch2,

1hdc into each of next 9 sts, turn.

151st – 153rd rows Work to end. Turn.

154th row Sl st over first 3 sts, ch2, work 1hdc into each of next 3 sts, turn.

155th row Work a loop st into each of these 3 sts. Fasten off.

Face

Using size H hook and A, ch4.

1st row 1sc into 2nd ch from hook, 1sc into each of next 2ch. Turn.

2nd row Ch 1, 1sc into each sc to end. Turn.

3rd row Inc 3 sts by working 4ch, sl st into 2nd ch from hook, sl st into each of next 2ch, 1sc into each sc to end. Turn.

4th row Inc 3 sts by working 4ch, 1sc into 2nd ch from hook, 1sc into each of next 2ch, 1sc into each sc and sl st to end. Turn.

5th and 6th rows Ch 1, 1sc into each st to end. Turn. 9sc.

7th row As 3rd row.

8th row Inc 6 sts by working 7ch, 1sc into 2nd ch from hook, 1sc into each st to end. Turn. 18sc.

9th and 10th rows Ch 1, 1sc into each st to end. Turn.

11th row As 4th row. 21sc.

12th – 14th rows Ch 1, 1sc into each st to end. Turn.

15th row Ch 1, 1sc into each of next 18sc, turn.

16th row Ch 1, 1sc into each st to end. Turn.

17th row As 3rd row.

18th row Sl st over first 3 sts, ch1, 1sc into each st to end. Turn. 18sc.

19th and 20th rows Ch 1, 1sc into each st to end. Turn.

21st row As 3rd row.

22nd and 23rd rows Ch 1, 1sc into each st to end. Turn.

24th row Inc 2 sts as for 4th row, work to within last st, inc in last st by working 2sc into last st. Turn. 24sc.

25th row Ch 1, 1sc in each st to end. Turn.

26th row Ch 1, dec one st by working 2 sts tog, 1 sc into each st to within last st, inc in last st. Turn.

27th row Ch 1, inc one st, 1sc into each st to end. Turn.

28th row Ch 1, dec one st, 1sc into each st to within last st, inc one st. Turn.

29th row Ch 1, inc one st, 1sc into each sc to within last 2sc, dec one st. Turn.

30th row Ch 1, dec one st, 1sc into each st to end. Turn.

31st row Ch 1, 1sc into each st to within last 2 sts, dec one st. Turn.

32nd row Ch 1, dec one st, 1sc into each st to end. Turn.

33rd row Ch 1, 1sc into each st to within last 2 sts, dec one st. Turn.

34th – 39th rows Rep 32nd and 33rd rows 3 times.

40th row Ch 1, dec one st, 1sc into each st to end. Turn.

41st row Ch 1, 1sc into each st to within last 2 sts, dec one st. Turn.

42nd row Ch 1, dec one st, 1sc into each st to within last 2 sts, dec one st. Turn.

43rd row As 42nd.

44th row Ch 1, dec one st, 1sc into each st to end. Fasten off.

Ear

Using size H hook and A, ch11.

1st row 1sc into 2nd ch from hook, 1sc into each ch to end. Turn.

Cont in sc, inc one st at each end of next 7 rows. 24 sts.

Work 6 rows sc without shaping.

Now dec one sc at each end of next and foll 8 alt rows ending with a row of sc.

Next row Ch 1, (dec 1 sc) twice. Turn.

Next row Work 2sc tog. Fasten off.

Tail

Using size H hook and A, ch22.

1st row 1hdc into 3rd ch from hook, 1hdc into each ch to end. Turn.

2nd row Work one 8ch loop into each st to end. Turn. 20 loops.

3rd row Ch 2, 1hdc into each of next 15hdc, turn.

4th row As 2nd row. 15 loops.

5th row Ch 2, 1hdc into each of next 10hdc, turn.

6th row As 2nd row. 10 loops.

7th row Ch 2, 1hdc into each of next 5hdc, turn.

8th row As 2nd row. 5 loops. Fasten off.

To finish

Darn in all ends.

Matching shapes carefully, sew face to body and body to grass section. Sew 4in of tail to body. Fold ear in half and sew top to face. Embroider eye in Satin stitch and nose and mouth in Stem stitch as shown in picture.

Alternatives

Change the look of the lamb with different loop stitches or use loops to make rugs or pillows.

Loop stitches in any of a number of styles, sizes and materials can add warmth and a woolly look and feel to any single crochet fabric. You can cover the whole fabric with loops for a cozy rug by the side of your bed or in the bathroom or you can cover part of the fabric with them — a woolly bear or a soft angora rabbit on a plain pillow cover, for example.

Loop stitches require a great deal of yarn. To be sure you have enough to finish your project, use a whole ball to work your chosen loop stitch pattern and then make a rough calculation of the amount of yarn you will need.

Loop-stitch patterns

1 Long-stitch loops

Extra long stitches worked alternately with single crochet form a thick, single-looped fabric.

Make an even number of ch.

Base row 1sc into 2nd ch from hook, 1sc into each ch to end. Turn.

1st row (WS) Ch1, 1sc into first st, * yo 8 times, insert hook into next st, yo and draw through a loop, (yo and draw through first 2 loops on hook) 9 times — loop st formed —, 1sc into next st, rep from * to end. Turn.

2nd row Ch 1 to count as first sc, skip first st, 1sc into each st to end. Turn.

1st and 2nd rows form pat. Rep them throughout.

2

2 Cut "fur" fabric

In this method the "fur" is attached after the background fabric has been worked. This can be somewhat tedious to do, but does enable you to make the fur from unusual yarns such as coarse string which would be difficult to work with in the normal way.

Background Use 2 yarns, A and B. Using A, make an even number of ch.

Base row 1sc into 4th ch from hook, *ch1, skip next ch, 1sc into next ch, rep from * to end. Turn.

Pat row Ch 2, *1sc into next ch sp, ch1, rep from * ending with 1sc into first turning ch. Turn.

Rep pat row for length required. Fasten off.

"Fur" Using B, cut strands of yarn approx twice the length required for the fur — here the cut lengths were 3in long.

*Insert hook around 2nd sc of base row from front to back, fold cut lengths in half, loop over the hook and draw them from left to right behind sc and to front of work, wind cut lengths around hook and draw through the loops on hook to knot the strands, pull cut ends to neaten the knot, rep from * for each sc, omitting first and last sts of each row. Trim pile and brush if applicable.

Padded futon

**This comfortable Japanese-style lounging mat is designed
for the beach, deck or yard. Its lightness and flexibility
make it especially easy to roll up and carry.**

Size
Approx 32½in × 67in

Gauge
16sc and 20 rows to 4in over pat on
size F crochet hook
To save time, check your gauge.

Materials
Approx 15oz each of a machine
washable sport or double knitting yarn
in colors (A) and (B)
38½in × 70in piece of cotton backing
fabric for lining
2½yds of heavyweight synthetic batting
2¼yds tape for ties
Size F crochet hook

Squares
Using A and size F crochet hook, ch47.
Base row 1sc into 2nd ch from hook,
1sc into each ch to end, turn. 46sc.
1st row Ch 1, skip 1st st, 1sc into
each sc to end, turn.
Rep the 1st row 56 times. Do not turn
at end of last row. Ch1, 1sc into same
sp as last st. Then work 43sc evenly
down side of square, ch1. 1sc into
same sp as last st, 43sc along base ch,
ch1, 1sc into same sp as last st, 43sc
evenly up to other side. Fasten off.
Make 8 more squares in A and 9 in B.

To finish
Press each square. Arrange the
squares so that the colors alternate and
the direction of the rows of stitches
also alternate. Sew them together with
an invisible seam (see page 153).
Place lining on top of the crochet, right
sides together, and sew the lining to
the crochet on three sides. Turn right
side out and insert the batting. On the
open side, turn under the seam
allowance on the lining and slipstitch it
to the crochet.
Baste the three layers together with
vertical and horizontal lines of stitches.
The lines of stitching should be just
under four inches apart and should
divide each crochet square into nine
equal sections. Machine or hand quilt

along the lines of basting. Work a second row of quilting across the width of the mat a third of the way down its length and again two-thirds of the way down.

Divide the tape in half and sew the halves to the ends of the mat, slightly off center. To fasten, fold in half, roll up and tie.

Alternatives

You can use padding and quilting with crochet whenever you want softness, thickness or warmth.

Choose one of our alternative patterns to make a soft cotton mat for your chaise or thick pads to protect your table from hot dishes. Or use wool to make an extra warm baby blanket for the stroller. To reduce bulk, use a light or medium-weight batting. If you plan to wash padded crochet, make sure that the yarn, backing and batting are all washable and that the yarn and backing are colorfast. See Padded work on page 163.

1 Crochet quilting

Quilting can be worked successfully with surface slip stitch. Place lightweight batting between two pieces of crochet — thicker batting would make it more difficult for the hook to pass through all three layers. Baste along the quilting lines. Work surface slip stitch (see page 157) through all three layers to quilt the fabric.

Note: It is possible to use surface slip stitch to work abstract designs.

2 Single crochet seaming

Narrow strips of padded crochet can be joined with single crochet.

Work a row of sc evenly around each piece of crochet and cut the batting as on page 163. Join the two pieces together to enclose the batting, inserting the hook under both loops on each edge.

Join the padded pieces together with single crochet, inserting the hook as before. The ridge produced can be used either on the WS or RS.

3 Backstitch quilting

Quilting by hand, though more time-consuming, produces as good results as machine quilting. Baste the lining, batting and crochet together as for machine quilting. Then, with right side facing, backstitch along the basted lines.

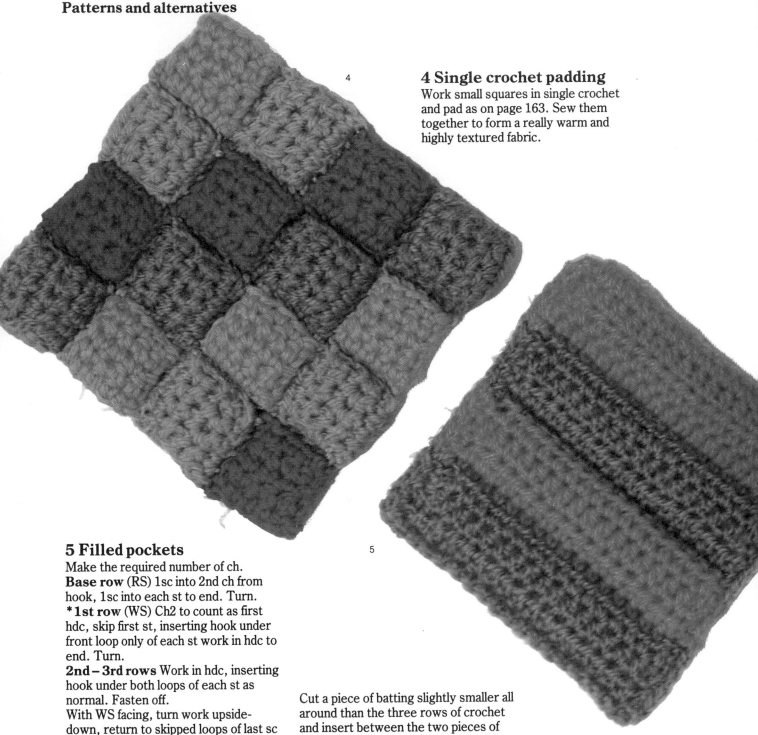

4

4 Single crochet padding

Work small squares in single crochet and pad as on page 163. Sew them together to form a really warm and highly textured fabric.

5

5 Filled pockets

Make the required number of ch.
Base row (RS) 1sc into 2nd ch from hook, 1sc into each st to end. Turn.
*1st row (WS) Ch2 to count as first hdc, skip first st, inserting hook under front loop only of each st work in hdc to end. Turn.
2nd – 3rd rows Work in hdc, inserting hook under both loops of each st as normal. Fasten off.
With WS facing, turn work upside-down, return to skipped loops of last sc row and rejoin yarn to first unworked loop.
Next row Ch 2 to count as first hdc, skip first st, 1hdc into each unworked loop to end. Turn.
Next 2 rows Work in hdc, inserting hook under both loops of each st in the usual way.

Cut a piece of batting slightly smaller all around than the three rows of crochet and insert between the two pieces of crochet. Fold the first 3 rows up to the last row worked.
Next row Work a row of sc, inserting the hook under both loops of the two edges. Turn.*
Rep from * to * for length required. Finish the edges by working a row of sc through both thicknesses of crochet.

Note: Increase the width of the pockets by working in double crochet or by working more rows, but always end each pocket on a wrong-side row.

Bedroom and bathroom accessories

White squared bedspread

This bedspread in silky, medium-weight cotton yarn looks and feels luxurious and will last for years.

Size
Overall size is approx 90in × 70in

Gauge
Each square measures 7in × 7in worked on size E hook
To save time, check your gauge.

Materials
About 5½lb of a size 3 crochet cotton
Size E crochet hook

To make a square
Using size E hook, ch8, sl st into first ch to form a ring.
1st round Ch 3, 15dc into ring, join with a sl st to 3rd of first 3ch. 16 sts.
2nd round Ch 5, *1dc into next dc, ch2, rep from * to end, join with a sl st to 3rd of first 5ch.
3rd round Ch 4, *3dc into next sp, ch1, rep from * to last sp, 2dc into next sp, join with a sl st to 3rd of first 4ch.
4th round *(1sc into 1ch sp, ch3) 3 times, 1sc into 1ch sp, ch6, rep from * 3 times more, join with a sl st to first sc.
5th round Ch 4, *(3dc into 3ch sp, ch1) 3 times, (5dc, ch2, 5dc) into 6ch sp, ch1, rep from * twice more, (3dc into 3ch sp, ch1) 3 times, (5dc, ch2, 4dc) into 6ch sp, join with a sl st to 3rd of first 4ch.
6th round *(1sc into 1ch sp, ch3) 4 times, 1sc into 4th of 5dc, ch6, 1 sc into 2nd of next 5dc, ch3, rep from * 3 times more, join with a sl st to first sc.
7th round Ch 4, (3dc into 3ch sp, ch1) 4 times, *(5dc, ch2, 5dc) into 6ch sp, ch1, (3dc into 3ch sp, ch1) 5 times, rep from * twice more, (5dc, ch2, 5dc) into 6ch sp, ch1, 2dc into 3ch sp, join with a sl st to 3rd of first 4ch.
8th round (1sc into 1 ch sp, ch3) 5 times, *1sc into 4th of 5dc, ch6, 1sc into 2nd of next 5dc, ch3, (1sc into 1ch sp, ch3) 6 times, rep from * twice more, 1sc into 4th of 5dc, ch6, 1sc into 2nd of next 5dc, ch3, 1sc into 1 ch sp, 3ch, join with a sl st to first sc.
9th round Ch 3, (3dc into 3ch sp) 5 times, * (5dc, ch2, 5dc) into 6ch sp, (3dc into 3ch sp) 7 times, rep from * twice more, (5dc, ch2, 5dc) into 6ch sp, 3dc into 3ch sp, 2dc into next 3ch sp, sl st to 3rd of first 3ch.
10th round Ch 3, 1dc into each dc all around and (1dc, 1tr, 1dc) into 2ch sp at each corner, end with sl st into 3rd of first 3ch. Fasten off.
Make a total of 130 squares in the same way.

Finishing
Overcast or crochet squares together into 13 strips of 10. Then join the strips. With RS facing, work a round of dc all around, working (2dc, 1tr, 2dc) into the tr at each corner. Turn.
Next round With WS facing, work in hdc all around, working 5hdc into the tr at each corner. Fasten off. Press work with a warm iron over a damp cloth.

Alternatives

The familiar granny square and other squares made in the round are among the most versatile and easiest of all forms of crochet.

One of the great advantages of squares is that you make them one at a time. You need not carry the whole bedspread or afghan with you to work on it. You can carry just enough yarn for two or three squares and work on them whenever you have a free moment. And, if you make a mistake, you need rip out only one square. There are many different patterns to choose from. You can make lacy ones for elegance or more solid ones for a casual look, or you can combine them. You can also make these squares in colors — one allover color or blocks of color for a patchwork effect. Or you can change the color several times within one square as is usually done in granny square afghans. And you can use almost any yarn. In fact multi-colored squares are good projects for using up leftover yarn. If you use a variety of yarns, however, make sure they all work to the same gauge. Squares can be used not only for bedspreads and afghans, but also to cover pillows or for mats. You can even put eight small ones together to make a tea cozy. Use four on each side, gather the top with a cord and leave openings at the sides for the handle and the spout.

If you do make a bedspread or afghan, see Finishing an afghan on page 153. You may want to finish the edges with two or three rows of single or double crochet. You can also add a fringe if you like.

Patterns and alternatives

Square Patterns

1 Granny square

Ch6, join with a sl st into first ch to form a ring.

1st round Ch 3, 2dc into ring, ch3, *3dc, ch3, rep from * twice more, join with a sl st to 3rd of 3ch.

2nd round Sl st into first 3ch sp, (ch3, 2dc, ch3, 3dc) into sp, *ch1 (3dc, ch3, 3dc) into next 3ch sp, rep from * twice more, ch1, join with a sl st to 3rd of 3ch.

3rd round Sl st into first 3ch sp, (ch3, 2dc, ch3, 3dc) into this sp, *ch1, 3dc into next 1ch sp, ch1, (3dc, ch3, 3dc) into next 3ch sp, rep from * ending

with ch1, 3dc into next 1 ch sp, ch1, join with a sl st to 3rd of 3ch.

4th round Sl st into first 3ch sp, (ch3, 2dc, ch3, 3dc) into this sp, *(ch1, 3dc into next 1ch sp) twice, ch1, (3dc, ch3, 3dc) into corner 3ch sp, rep from * — ending last rep (ch1, 3dc into next 1 ch sp) twice, ch1, join with a sl st to 3rd of 3ch.

5th round Sl st into first 3ch sp, (ch3, 2dc, ch3, 3dc) into this sp, *(ch1, 3dc into next 1 ch sp) 3 times, ch1, (3dc,

ch3, 3dc) into corner 3ch sp, rep from * ending last rep (ch1, 3dc into next 1 ch sp) 3 times, ch1, join with a sl st to 3rd of first 3ch. Cont working rounds in this way, with 1 more group of doubles between each corner until square is required size.

2 Crossed square

Ch8, join with a sl st into first ch to form a ring.

1st round Ch 3, (yo, insert hook into ring, yo, draw 1 loop through, yo, draw

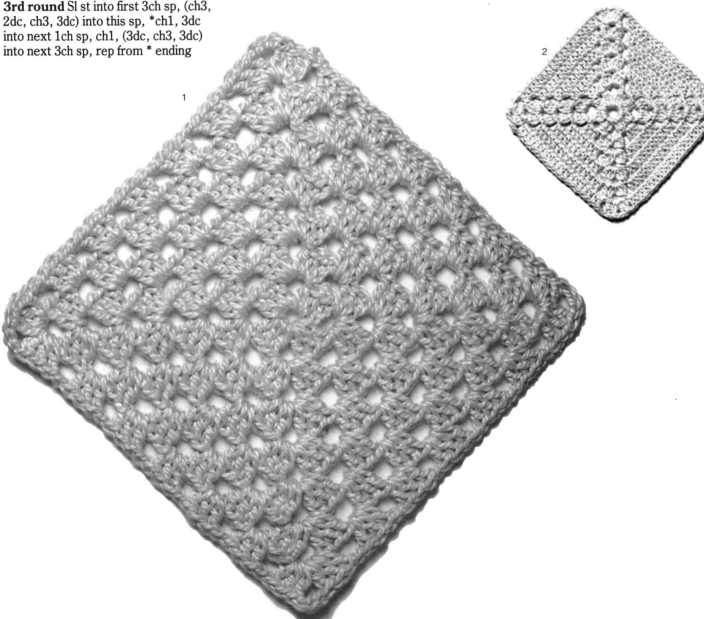

94

2 loops through) twice, yo, draw 3 loops through — ½ cluster formed —, ch5, (yo, insert hook into ring, yo, draw 1 loop through, yo, draw 2 loops through) 3 times, yo, draw 4 loops through — 1 cluster formed —, ch2, *1 cluster, ch5, 1 cluster, ch2, rep from * twice more, sl st to 3rd of 3ch.

2nd round Sl st into first 5ch sp, ch3, ½ cluster into next 5ch sp, ch2, 1 cluster into same sp, ch2, 3dc into next 2ch sp, ch2, *(1 cluster, ch2, 1 cluster) into next 5ch sp, ch2, 3dc into next 2ch sp, ch2, rep from * to end, join with a sl st to 3rd of 3ch.

3rd round Sl st into next st, ch3, *(1 cluster, ch2, 1 cluster) into next 2ch sp (corner made), ch2, 2dc into next 2ch sp, 1 dc into each of next 3dc, 2dc into next 2ch sp, ch2, rep from * to end, join with sl st to 3rd of 3ch. Cont working dc into dc of last row, clusters at corners and 2dc into 2ch sp at side of each corner, until required size.

3 Center wheel
Ch8, join with a sl st into first ch to form a ring.

1st round Ch 3, 15dc into ring, join with a sl st to 3rd of 3ch.

2nd round Ch 5, *1dc into next dc, ch2, rep from * to end, join with a sl st to 3rd of first 5ch. 16dc.

3rd round Ch 3, 2dc into first 2ch sp, ch1, *(3dc, ch1) into next 2ch sp, rep from * to end, join with a sl st to 3rd of 3ch.

4th round *(ch3, 1sc into next 1 ch sp) 3 times, ch6, 1sc into corner sp, rep from * to end, join with a sl st to first of 3ch.

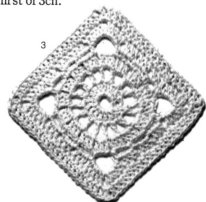

5th round Ch 3, 2dc into first 3ch sp, 3dc into each of next 2 3ch sp, * (5dc, ch2, 5dc) into corner sp, 3dc into each of next 3ch sp, rep from * twice more, (5dc, ch2, 5dc) into last corner sp, join with a sl st to 3rd of 3ch.

6th round Ch 3, 1 dc into each dc all around and (1dc, 1tr, 1dc) into each 2ch sp at corner, join with a sl st to 3rd of 3ch. Fasten off.

4 Square center
Ch10, join with a sl st into first ch to form a ring.

1st round Ch 10, *4tr into ring, ch7, rep from * twice more, 3tr into ring, join with a sl st to 3rd of first 10ch. Sl st into each of next 3ch. Turn work.

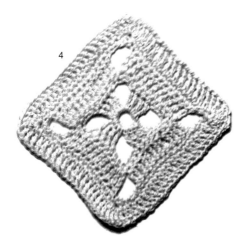

2nd round *1sc into each of next 10 sts, skip next st, rep from * to end, join with a sl st to first sc.

3rd round Ch 10, 2tr into first sc, 1 tr into each of next 8sc, 2tr into next sc, 7ch, (2tr into next sc, 1tr into each of next 8sc, 2tr into next sc, 7ch) twice, 2tr into next sc, 1tr into each of next 9sc, join with a sl st to 3rd of first 10ch. Sl st over 3ch, turn work.

4th round *1sc into each of next 18sc, skip 1 sc, rep from * to end, join with a sl st to first sc.

5th round Ch 3, * 6tr into corner st, 1 tr into each st to next corner, rep from * to end, join with a sl st to 3rd of 3ch. Fasten off.

5 Squared circle
Ch 12, join with a sl st into first ch to form a ring.

1st round Ch 5, *1tr into ring, ch1, rep from * 14 times more. Sl st to 4th of first 5ch.

2nd round Ch 4, 3dc into first ch sp, drop loop from hook, insert hook into top of first 4ch and through dropped loop, draw loop through, ch2, *4dc into next 1ch sp, drop loop from hook, insert hook into top of first of 4dc and through dropped loop, draw loop through, ch2, rep from * 14 times more, join with a sl st to 4th of 4ch.

3rd round Sl st into first 2ch sp, ch3, (3dc, ch2, 4dc) into same sp, * (ch3, 1sc into next 2ch sp) 3 times, ch3, (4dc, ch2, 4dc) into next 2ch sp, rep from * twice more, (ch3, 1sc into next 2ch sp) 3 times, join with a sl st to 3rd of 3ch.

4th round Sl st into first 2ch corner sp, ch3, (3dc, ch2, 3dc) into same sp, *(4dc into next 1 ch sp) 3 times, 4dc ch2, 4dc into next corner sp, rep from * twice more, (4dc into next 1 ch sp) 3 times, join with a sl st to 3rd of 3ch. Fasten off.

Lace-trimmed sheets

Make pretty edgings in cotton to dress up plain sheets and pillowcases. Use white trim on colored sheets or colored trim on white.

Size

Edging measures approx 2¾in at its deepest point

Gauge

12 pairs of dc on base measure 4in in length
To save time, check your gauge.

Materials

To edge one standard single-bed sheet and pillowcase:
Approx 285yds of a size 3 crochet cotton
Size B crochet hook

Sheet edging

Base Using size B hook, ch7, 1dc into 6th ch from hook, 1dc into last ch, turn, *ch5, 1dc into each of next 2dc, turn *, rep from * to * for width of sheet, so that total number of 5ch loops on each edge of base is divisible by 4. Work from * to * once more, sl st into next dc and into first 3ch of first 5ch loop.
1st row (RS) 1sc into same place as last sl st, *ch4, 1sc into next 5ch loop, ch1, 7dc into next 5ch loop, ch1, 1sc into next 5ch loop, ch4, 1sc int next 5ch loop, rep from * to end. Turn.
2nd row Ch 1, 1sc into first ch, *4sc into next 4ch loop, ch1 (1dc into next dc, ch1) 7 times, 4sc into next 4ch loop, 1sc into next sc, rep from * to end, ending last rep with 1sc into last sc. Turn.
3rd row Ch 1, skip first sc, 1sc into each of next 3sc, *ch2, (1dc into next dc, ch1) 6 times, 1dc into next dc, ch2, skip next 2sc, 1sc into each of next 5sc, rep from * to end, ending last rep with skip next 2sc, 1sc into each of next 3sc. Turn.
4th row Ch 3, *(1dc into next dc, ch2) 7 times, 1sc into 3rd of next 5sc, ch2,

rep from * to end, ending last rep with 1sc into last sc. Turn.
5th row Ch 4, *1tr into next dc, ch2, (1tr into next dc, ch3, sl st to top of tr just worked, ch2) 5 times, 1tr into next dc, rep from * to end, ch4, sl st to first of 3 turning ch at beg of 4th row.
Fasten off.
Inner edge With RS facing, rejoin yarn to top of first dc on other edge of base, ch6, *1sc into next 5ch loop, ch4, rep from * to end, ch6, sl st to base of last dc.
Fasten off.

Pillowcase edging

Work as for Sheet edging, but rep Base from * to * for width of pillowcase.
1st – 5th rows and inner edge
Work as for Sheet edging.

To finish

Using rustproof steel pins, pin the edging to correct size and dampen it lightly. Allow to dry and then sew to sheet and pillowcase (see Stab stitch, page 154).

Alternatives

Use intricate combinations of bobbles, picots, fans and shells to add a touch of decorative individuality to sheets, pillowcases, towels, napkins and tablecloths.

The majority of the alternative edgings are formed on a base worked lengthwise on a few foundation chains. Following rows are then worked along one or both long sides of the base. There is no need to measure the article you are trimming before you begin to

work. Instead, work the base until it is long enough to fit exactly the article you are decorating.

Varying effects

The appearance of the edgings can be varied greatly by changing the color or thickness of the yarn used.
We have used medium cotton for the edgings on the bed linen shown opposite; it gives a fairly solid effect. Worked in a finer cotton or even a glitter yarn, the effect would be very different.
Most of these edgings look best when worked in a color that contrasts with the article. This allows the intricate loops, bobbles and clusters of the edging to be seen clearly.
A softer effect could be achieved by working the edging in exactly the same color as the article.

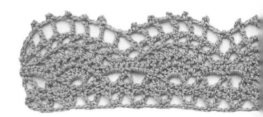

Decorative edgings

1 Narrow picot edging

Work base as required so that right-hand edge begins and ends with a 5ch loop. Turn and beg picot row, worked into edge of base.

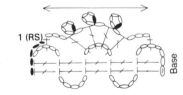

2 Double bobble edging

Work bobbles (see Simple bobble edging below) on base from 4dc, and end with 5ch, (1dc, ch2, 1dc) into 2ch sp. After 1st row fasten off and, with RS facing, work 2nd row into other edge of base.

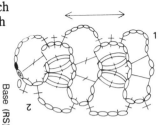

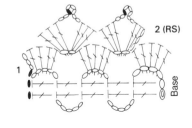

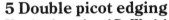

3 Wide looped edging

Beg with 12ch and after working the base, rep 1st and 2nd rows as required. Do not turn, but work edging into left-hand edge of base.

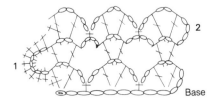

5 Double picot edging

Use 2 colors, A and B. Work base in A as for Narrow picot edging. After 1st row in A fasten off and with RS facing use B to work 2nd row into other edge of base.

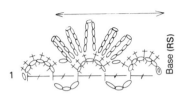

4 Looped edging

Work base as required, ending with odd number of 5ch loops. Work loop row into edge of base with RS facing.

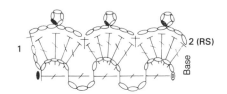

Lace-trimmed sheets

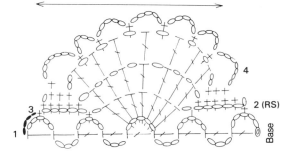

6 Double block edging

Work base as required and turn. Work 1st and 2nd rows into edge of base.

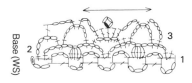

7 Narrow bobbled edging

Work base as required so that number of sps divides by 4, plus 1. Work bobbles (see page 156) from 5dc.

8 Simple bobble edging

Base Work as for base of Narrow picot edging.

1st row Ch 7, 1sc into first 5ch loop, *ch5, 1sc into same loop, ch7, 1sc into next 5ch loop, rep from * to end. Turn.
2nd row (RS) Ch 5, *2sc into next 7ch loop, ch2, 4dc into next 5ch loop, remove hook from loop and insert it into first dc just worked, insert hook into loop just dropped and draw through all loops on hook — bobble formed —, ch2, rep from * ending with 2sc into last 7ch loop. Fasten off.

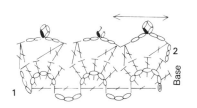

9 Shell picot edging

Use 2 colors, A and B. Work base in A. Turn and work 1st row into edge. Fasten off and work 2nd row in B.

10 Fan edging

Work base so that number of 5ch loops divides by 3 plus 2.

99

Fabric and crochet bedspread

Combine fabric and crochet to make a different kind of patchwork bedspread. You can buy fabric to match your room or use a variety of scraps or remnants.

Size

83in wide by 96½in long, to fit a double bed

Materials

Approx 2,660yds of a size 3 crochet cotton
42 squares of fabric each 13in × 13in
Size E crochet hook
Large-eyed embroidery needle

To prepare a square

Turn a ⅝in hem to wrong side on two opposite sides of the square. Turn under the raw edges and baste in place. Then turn under ⅝in hems on the remaining two sides in the same way and baste. Machine stitch with matching thread. The squares can be interfaced and lined if you wish. You will need extra material for the lining

and interfacing. Cut lining squares the same size as the unfinished original squares. Cut interfacing squares ⅝in smaller all around. Baste interfacing to center of wrong side of original squares. Place original squares on top of lining squares, right sides together. Baste on three sides and machine stitch ⅝in from edge. Trim seam allowances and turn right side out. Fold seam allowances on fourth side to the inside and, with matching thread, slip stitch together. Press on the wrong side. Following the Special technique given below, and using crochet thread and embroidery needle, work blanket stitches all around the edges of the squares.
Making the stitches all the same length, work 48 sts along each side and 3 sts at each corner. Work evenly,

paying attention to the looped edge of the stitch: this forms the foundation for the edging.

Edging

Join yarn to first st at one corner and using the crochet hook ch1 to count as first sc, *2sc into last loop at corner, 2sc into first loop on next side, 1sc into each loop of next side, rep from * all around, sl st into first ch.
Next round Ch2 to count as first dc, keeping hook at front of work, work 1dc into st before sl st — 2dc crossed —, skip next st, 1dc into next st, keeping hook at front of work, work 1dc into st that was skipped — 2dc crossed —, work 2dc, 1ch and 2dc into corner st, *(work 2 crossed dc) to next corner st, 2dc, ch1 and 2dc all into corner st, rep from * twice more,

Special technique — blanket stitch edging

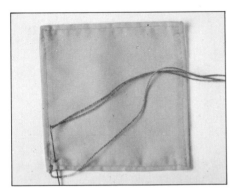

1 *With right side facing and working from left to right, fasten the thread to the back about ¼in from the side and bottom edges. Bring the thread over the bottom edge, insert it from front to back about ¼in above the edge and bring it through the loop at the bottom edge to make the first blanket stitch.*

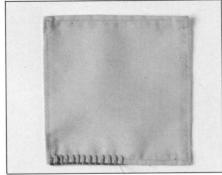

2 *Insert the needle from front to back again, approximately ¼in to right of the last stitch, bring it through loop at the edge and draw up the thread along the edge being careful not to pull the fabric out of shape. Continue in this way to the corner.*

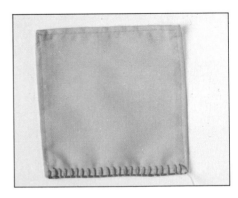

3 *To turn corner, work one blanket stitch ¼in from the corner and then another into the same place. Work the same number of stitches on each side of the square. Complete last corner in the same way and then draw the thread through first horizontal loop and fasten at the back of work.*

(work 2 crossed dc) to end, sl st into top of 3ch.

Next round As last round, working 2dc, ch1 and 2dc into space at corners. Fasten off.

Edge all squares in the same way.

To finish

Arrange squares, wrong side up, in pattern of your choice — we have alternated dark- and light-colored squares — to form a rectangle 6 squares wide by 7 squares long. Overcast the squares together catching the loops on corresponding stitches.

Border

With RS of work facing, join yarn to first 2 crossed dc on one side, 1sc into same place as join, (skip next dc, 5dc into next dc, skip next dc, 1sc into next dc) to corner, rep from * to corner, work * 7dc into space at corner, (skip next dc, 5dc into next dc, skip next dc, 1sc into next dc) to corner, rep from * 3 times more, sl st into first sc. Fasten off. Press fabric.

"Sleep well" sheets

Trim sheets with a long strip of white filet, saying "Sleep well" in three languages.

Sizes

To fit single [double] sheet
Depth of trim 5½in
Length of trim 71[90½]in
Length of lettered panel 35½[50]in

Note: Directions for the larger size are in square brackets [ ]; where there is only one set of figures, it applies to both sizes.

Gauge

10½ spaces and 11 rows to 2in worked over plain filet mesh
To save time, check your gauge.

Materials

885[1239]yds of a size 20 crochet cotton
Size 7 steel crochet hook

Note: See Filet crochet on page 161.

Single-sheet trim

Using size 7 steel hook, ch83.
Base row 1dc into 8th ch from hook, (ch2, skip next 2ch, 1dc into next ch) 4 times, 1dc into each of next 6ch, (ch2, skip next 2ch, 1dc into next ch) 19 times. Turn.
1st row (WS) ch5, skip first dc, (1dc into next dc, ch2) 17 times, 1dc into next dc, 2dc into next sp, 1dc into next dc, (ch2, skip next 2dc, 1dc into next dc) twice, 2dc into next sp, 1dc into next dc, (ch2, 1dc into next dc) 3 times, ch2, 1dc into last sp. Turn.
Last row forms 18 sps, 1 block, 2 sps, 1 block, 4 sps.
2nd row 5 sps, 2 blocks, 19 sps. Turn.
3rd row 18 sps, 1 block, 2 sps, 1 block, 4 sps. Turn.
Rep 1st and 2nd rows until a total of 90 rows have been worked from beg. Then work 180 rows of chart, beg 1st

row at edge marked with an arrow. Work 90 rows to match those worked at beg of trim, ending with a WS row. Turn and do not fasten off.

Picot edging

(3sc, ch3, sl st to top of last sc — picot formed) into each sp to end. Fasten off.

Single-crochet edging

With RS facing, rejoin yarn to first sp on opposite edge of trim, work 3sc into each sp to end. Fasten off.

Double-sheet trim

Work base and 1st–2nd rows as for single-sheet trim. Then rep 1st and 2nd rows until 104 rows have been worked from beg.
Work 252 rows of the chart, beg 1st row at the edge marked with an arrow. Work 104 rows to match those worked

---

Special technique — graphing filet letters

1 *Using tracing paper and a soft pencil, trace the outline of the letter — it could be taken from a book, magazine or your own design. Turn the paper over and carefully trace the outline of the letter as shown.*

2 *Turn back to the first side of the paper and stick the tracing to graph paper with masking tape to prevent slipping. Using a soft pencil, shade over the outline of the letter. The shape of the letter should appear on the graph paper.*

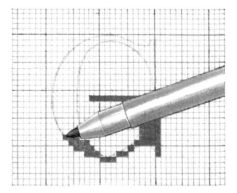

3 *Remove the masking tape and tracing paper. Shade the squares of graph paper that are within the outline of the letter and those that are partly inside the outline to obtain a good shape. When working the filet, the shaded areas will be blocks and the clear areas will be mesh.*

at beg of trim, ending with a WS row. Complete as for single.

To finish

Press work under a damp cloth. Place trim on sheet as shown in photograph and sew in place.

Alternatives

Use these Roman and Victorian alphabets to add a personal message to your sheets, pillowcases and other linens.

The charts on page 104 contain the alphabet in Roman capital letters. The chart on page 105 shows a Victorian alphabet. Either chart can be used with filet.

Monograms or complete words and phrases worked in filet crochet should be done carefully so they can be read easily. Use a fairly fine, untextured yarn like the number 20 cotton used for the "sleep well" sheet trims. The color of the trim should contrast strongly with that of the sheets — otherwise the words will not show up. Always remove the trim before washing the sheet.

Using the yarn of your choice, work a gauge swatch to check the number of spaces in a 4in square of filet mesh. Measure the length and width of the proposed filet fabric — for a pillow trim or curtain, for example.

Divide the length of the filet by 4in and multiply by the number of spaces to 4in on the length of the gauge sample. Calculate the number of spaces in the width the same way.

Patterns and alternatives

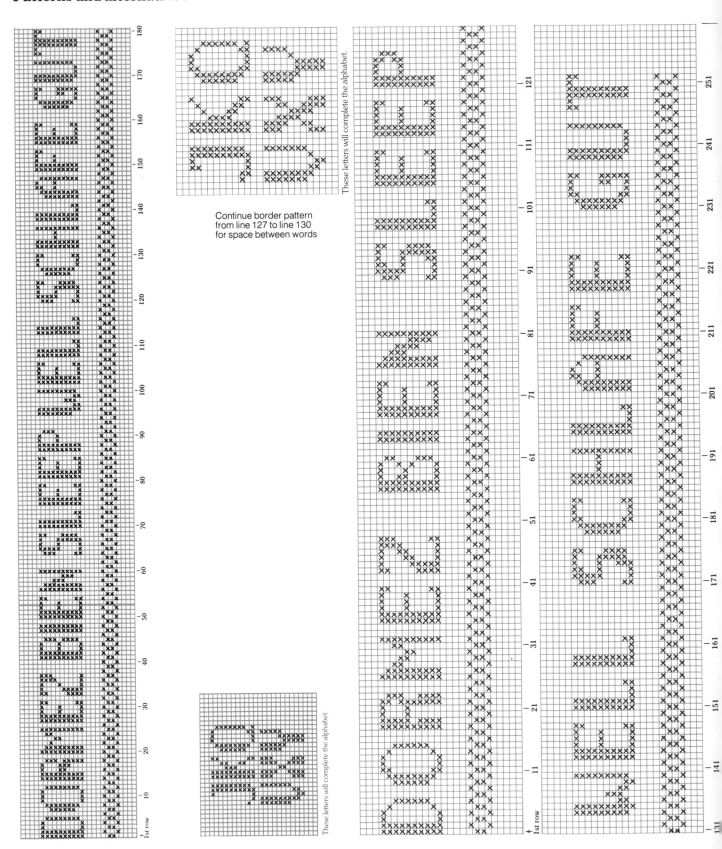

Continue border pattern
from line 127 to line 130
for space between words

These letters will complete the alphabet.

These letters will complete the alphabet.

Delicate filet bedspread

This beautiful bedspread worked in fine cotton makes an heirloom any family would be proud to own.

Size
Single 67in × 90½in
Double 75in × 90½in

Gauge
10 blocks/spaces and 14 rows to 4in
worked on size B hook
To save time, check your gauge.

Materials
7,320yds of a size 5 crochet cotton
Size B crochet hook

Note: See Working in fine cotton on page 14.

Note: Each block consists of 4 double crochets with 3 doubles worked for each additional block where they are side by side, and 2 chains for each space.

Bedspread

Single bed

1st row 1dc into 8th ch from hook, 1dc into each of next 36ch (ch2, skip 2ch, 1dc into next ch) 178 times, 1dc into each of next 36ch, ch2, skip 2ch, 1dc into last ch.

Double bed

1st row 1dc into 8th ch from hook, *ch2, skip 2ch, 1dc into next ch, rep from * to end.

← center

2nd row
1st row

single size

2nd row
1st row

double size

↑center

¼ section

Patterns and alternatives

Both sizes

Beginning from the 2nd row as indicated cont in pat from chart. When center of row is reached, work back in reverse to beg of row. Continue until half of the bedspread has been worked, then turn chart upside down and work 2nd half.

Borders

(make separately)

Single bed

Ch101, 1dc into 8th ch from hook, 1dc into each of next 3ch (ch2, skip 2ch, 1dc into next ch) 3 times, 1dc into each of next 3ch, (ch2, skip 2ch, 1dc into next ch) 4 times, 1dc into each of next 3ch (ch2, skip 2ch, 1dc into next ch) twice, 1dc into each of next 3ch, (ch2, skip 2ch, 1dc into next ch) 15 times, 1dc into each of last 9dc, turn.

Cont working in pattern from chart until long enough to reach along side edge of bedspread.

Before working the first corner, pin out and press the bedspread and border to make sure the border is the correct length. Adjust if necessary. To turn corner, decrease one space or block on inner edge of every row until only two blocks remain (see chart), then turn chart and complete corner by increasing one space or block on every row. Work along the end of the bedspread, turn the second corner and work 2nd side to match first.

Double bed

Ch84, 1dc into 4th ch from hook, 1dc into each of next 2ch (ch2, skip 2ch, 1dc into next ch), 8 times, 1dc into each of next 6dc, (ch2, skip 2ch, 1dc into next dc) 13 times, 1dc into each of next 9dc, turn.

Cont as given for single size, working along side edge, along end and then up other side.

To finish

Press border and bedspread.
Working on wrong side, and with matching thread, overcast border to bedspread matching blocks and spaces.

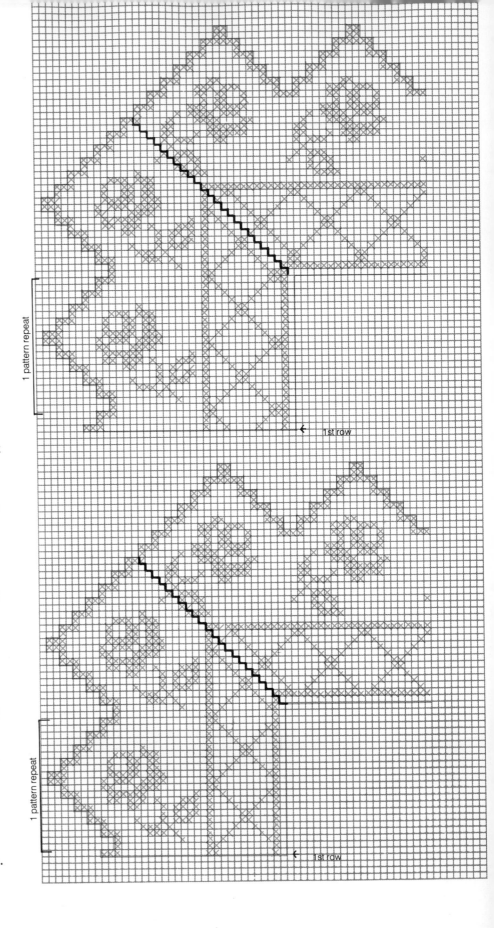

1 pattern repeat

1st row

1 pattern repeat

1st row

Trimmed towels

Make one or all of these pretty edgings and sew them to your towels to add an air of elegance and luxury to your bathroom.

Patterns and alternatives

First edging

Size
Depth of edging, approx 3in

Gauge
One section measures 2⅔in. For an edging measuring more or less than 16in, divide the length required by 2⅔in for the sections needed.
To save time, check your gauge.

Materials
Approx 165yds of a size 5 rayon crochet thread make two edgings for a towel 16in wide
Size 7 steel crochet hook

Section
Using size 7 steel hook ch13.
1st row 1dc into 9th ch from hook, ch4, 1sc into last ch. Turn.
2nd row Ch 3, 9dc into 4ch sp, 1dc into next dc, 9dc all into last ch sp, 1dc into 5th of the 8ch. Turn.

3rd row Ch 5, 1dc into 3rd dc, (ch2, skip next dc, 1dc into next dc) to end, working last dc into top of 3ch. Turn. (10 sps.)
4th row Ch 3, (3dc all into next 2ch sp, 1dc into next dc) to end, finishing 3dc all into last ch sp, 1dc into 3rd of the 5ch. Turn. 41 dc.
5th row As 3rd. 20 sps. Fasten off,

skip next dc, 1sc into next dc, sl st over next 2ch and into next dc, turn.
2nd row Work 10dc all into next 4ch sp, 1dc into next dc, 10dc all into next 4ch sp, sl st into next dc on first scallop, sl st over next 2ch and into next dc, turn, 21dc.
3rd row Ch 2, 1dc into dc, (ch2, skip next dc, 1dc into next dc) 8 times, ch2, sl st into next dc on first scallop, sl st over next 2ch and into next dc, turn.
4th row 3dc into next 2ch sp, (1dc into next dc, 3dc all into next 2ch sp) to end, sl st into next dc on first scallop, sl st over next 2ch and into next dc, turn.
5th row Ch 2, 1dc into 3rd dc, (ch2, skip next dc, 1dc into next dc) 18 times, ch2, sl st into next dc on first scallop. Fasten off, leaving a long end for joining sections. This completes one section. Make 5 more sections and join together for the length of 7 sps. Work 1 row of sc along top edge. Make another edging; stitch to towel.

leaving a long end for joining sections. This completes first scallop.
With WS of first scallop facing, work 1sc into the dc two to the right of the center dc, ch4, 1dc into center dc, ch4,

Second edging

Size
Depth of edging, approx 3in

Gauge
One section measures 3⅛in. For an edging measuring more or less than 16in, divide the length required by 3⅛in for the sections needed.

Materials
About 200yds of a size 5 rayon crochet thread make two edgings for a towel 16in wide
Size 7 steel crochet hook

Section
Using size 7 steel hook ch17.
1st row 1dc into 6th ch from hook, ch2, skip next 2ch, 1dc into each of next 6ch, ch2, skip next 2ch, 1dc into last ch. Turn.
2nd row Ch 5, 1dc into first dc, ch2, 1dc into each of next 6dc, ch2, 1dc into last dc. Turn.
3rd – 5th rows As 2nd.
6th row Ch 5, 1dc into first dc, ch2, 1dc into each of next 2dc, 1hdc into each of next 2 sts, 1sc into each of next 2 sts. Turn.
7th row Ch 1, 1sc into each of next 2 sts, 1hdc into each of next 2 sts, 1dc into each of next 2 sts, 2ch, 1dc into last dc. Turn.
8th – 17th rows Rep 6th and 7th rows 5 times.
18th row Ch 5, 1dc into first dc, ch2, 1dc into each of next 2 sts, 1hdc into each of next 2 sts, 1sc into each of next 2 sts, ch5, sl st into last inside 5ch loop on first side of section, turn.
19th row Ch 2, 1dc into 3rd of the 5ch, ch2, 1dc into each of next 2sc, 1dc into each of next 2hdc, 1dc into each of next 2dc, ch2, 1dc into last dc. Turn.
20th row Ch 5, 1dc into first dc, ch2, 1dc into each of next 6 sts, ch2, 1dc into last dc, ch2, sl st into next inside loop, turn.
21st row Ch 2, 1dc into first dc, ch2, 1dc into each of next 6 sts, ch2, 1dc into last dc. Turn.
22nd row As 21st.
23rd row As 22nd.
This completes first section. Do not

fasten off, but ch22, turn.
Next row 1dc into 6th ch from hook, ch2, skip next 2ch, 1dc into each of next 6ch, ch2, skip next 2ch, 1dc into next ch, turn leaving 5ch as join between 1st and 2nd section. Now rep 2nd to 23rd rows as 1st section, but join outside loops to previous section for first 3 loops thus: at end of next row ch2, sl st into loop on previous sections, ch2, turn and omit 5ch at beg of next row.
Cont to make sections in this way until there are 5 sections in all. Fasten off.
Make another edging; sew to towel.

Third edging

Size
Depth of edging, approx 2¼in

Materials
About 200yds of a size 5 rayon crochet thread make two edgings for a towel 16in wide
Size 7 steel crochet hook

To make
Using size 7 steel hook ch16, sl st into first ch to form a circle.
1st row Ch 1, 1sc into first ch, 2sc into each of next 12ch. Turn, leaving 3ch unworked. 25sc.
2nd row Ch 1, 1sc into each sc to end. Turn.
3rd row As 2nd.
4th row Ch 1, 1sc into each of first 3sc, (1sc into next sc, ch4, 1sc into same sc, 1sc into each of next 2sc) 7 times, 1sc into last sc. Turn.
5th row Ch 13, sl st into 2nd 4ch loop, turn.
6th row Ch 1, 1sc into first ch, 2sc into each of next 12ch, turn. 25sc.
7th and 8th rows As 2nd.
9th row As 4th.
10th row As 5th.
11th row As 6th.
12th row As 2nd.
13th row As 2nd, then sl st into 3rd 4ch loop of adjacent motif, turn.
The 9th to 13th rows form pat. Rep them for 16in, ending with a 9th row. Fasten off. Join "loose" edges of end shells to adjacent shells. Make another edging and stitch to towel.

Fourth edging

Size
Depth of edging, approx 2in

Gauge
One shell section measures 3⅛in. For an edging measuring more or less than 16in, divide the length required by 3⅛in for the number of shell sections needed, then multiply number of sections by 24ch, plus 5 for starting ch.

Materials
About 200yds of a size 5 rayon crochet thread make two edgings for a towel 16in wide
Size 7 steel crochet hook

To make
Using size 7 steel hook ch125.
1st row 1sc into 2nd ch from hook, 1sc into each ch to end. Turn.
2nd row Ch 5, 1dc into 4th sc, (ch2, skip next 2sc, 1dc into next sc) to end. Turn. 41 sps.
3rd row Ch 1, 1sc into first dc, (2sc into next 2ch sp, 1sc into next dc) 7 times. Turn. 22sc.
4th row Ch 16, skip first 7sc, 1sc into next sc, turn, 8sc, into 16ch sp, 1sc into 8th of the 16ch, turn, *ch10, 1sc into same sc on 3rd row, turn, 8sc into 10ch sp, 1sc into 8th of the 10ch, turn *, rep from * to * once, ch8, skip next 6sc on 3rd row, 1sc into next sc, turn.
5th row 11sc into next 8ch sp, 1sc into top of first branch, (4sc into next 2ch sp, 1sc into top of next branch) twice, 11sc into next 8ch sp, 2sc into next 2ch sp on 2nd row, 1sc into next dc, turn.
6th row 1dc into each of 33sc around shell, sl st into 3rd sc on 3rd row, turn.
7th row Sl st over first 4dc, (sl st into next dc, ch4, sl st into same dc, sl st over next 5dc) 5 times, working over 4dc instead of 5dc at end of last rep. Fasten off. This completes one shell. Rejoin yarn to next st on 2nd row and rep 3rd to 7th rows again.
Cont in this way until 5 shells are completed. Rejoin yarn to next st on 2nd row and work 2sc into end 5ch sp, 1sc into 3rd of the 5ch. Fasten off.
Make another edging; sew to towel.

Basket weave bathmat

This bathmat is just the thing for catching splashes and drips. It is worked in a thick cotton in a sturdy basket weave pattern and is trimmed on three sides with a fringe.

Size

Approx 16½in wide by 27in long, excluding fringe

Gauge

1 pat rep (12sts) to 2⅜in and 16 rows to 5⅛in over pat on size E hook
To save time, check your gauge.

Materials

Approx 15oz of a sport weight cotton yarn for mat; 4oz for fringe in a contrasting color, if preferred
Size E crochet hook

Note: See Working around the stem on page 149.

To make

Using size E hook ch 140.
Base row 1dc into 4th ch from hook. 1dc into each ch to end. Turn. Commence pat.
1st row (RS) Ch2, work around each of next 5dc by working yo, insert hook from front to back between next 2dc,

around dc at left and through work from back to front; draw yarn through and complete dc in usual way — called double around front (dc front) —, work around each of next 6dc by working yo, insert hook from back to front between next 2dc, around dc at left and through work from front to back; draw yarn through and complete dc in usual way — called 1 double around back (dc back) —, work *6dc front, 6dc back, rep from * to within last 6sts, dc front to end. Turn.

2nd row Ch2, work 5dc back, 6dc front, *6dc back, 6dc front, rep from * to within last 6sts, dc back to end. Turn.

3rd row As 1st row.
4th row As 1st row.
5th row As 2nd row.
6th row As 1st row.
These 6 rows form the pat. Rep them 7 times more, then work 1st to 3rd rows again.
Fasten off.

Fringe

Using four strands of yarn together, knot fringe into every alternate row end along each short edge and into every alternate st along one long edge. Trim the ends.

Alternatives

Use any of several basket weave stitches to produce a sturdy fabric with a woven look.

Basket weave looks more difficult than it is and can be used in a wide variety of yarns for many different purposes. Try it in a medium cotton for thick, protective, country-look place mats, use wool for a foot-warming rug beside your bed or use acrylic yarn to make a washable blanket to sit on for picnics. Buy one ball of the yarn you would like to use and try it in one or more of the stitches below to make sure the yarn and stitch together produce a fabric that is appropriate for the project you have in mind. Samples that do not work for one project may work for another. Keep them for reference.

Basket weave stitches

Elongated basket stitch

Work into the row two rows below, placing the hook between the stitches each time to make the long doubles. The pattern is worked over a number of chains divisible by 6, plus 3, with 2 extra for the turning chain.

1st row 1dc into 4th ch from hook, 1dc into each ch to end. Turn.
2nd row Ch1, skip first st, 1sc into each st to end. Turn.
3rd row (WS) Ch3, skip first st, 1dc into each of next 2 sts, *(yo and insert hook between next 2dc in row below, yo and draw yarn up to same height as row being worked, complete double in normal way — called 1dc below —) 3 times, 1dc into each of next 3 sts working into top of stitch in normal way — called 1dc top —, rep from * to end, working last dc into turning chain. Turn.
4th row (RS) As 2nd.
5th row Ch3, 1dc below between 1st

Elongated basket stitch

and 2nd dc in row below, 1dc below between next 2dc, *1dc top into each of next 3dc, (1dc below between next 2dc) 3 times, rep from * to end, working last dc below between last dc and turning chain. Turn.
6th row As 4th.
3rd to 6th rows form pat and are rep throughout.

Basket weave variation

This pattern has a definite right and wrong side to it. It is worked over a number of chains divisible by 10, plus 7, with 2 extra for the turning chain.

1st row (RS) 1dc into 4th ch from hook, 1dc into each ch to end. Turn.
2nd row Ch3, skip first dc, yo and insert hook from right to left from back to front, around stem of next dc and to back of work again, yo and draw through a loop, yo and draw through 2 loops, yo and draw through rem 2 loops — 1 double back —, 1dc back around each of next 4dc, *1dc into each of next 5dc in normal way, 1dc back around each of next 5dc, rep from * to end, 1dc into top of turning chain. Turn.

Patterns and alternatives

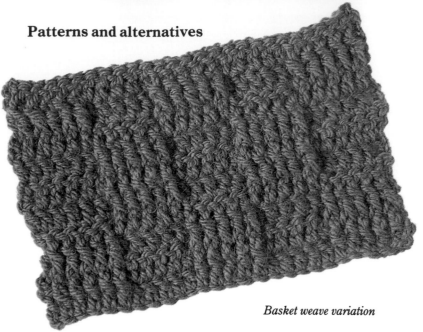

3rd row Ch 3, skip first dc, yo, insert hook between 2nd and 3rd dc, from front to back, around stem of next dc and to the front again, yo and draw through a loop, yo and draw through 2 loops on hook, yo and draw through rem 2 loops — 1 double front — around each of next 4dc, *1dc into each of next 5dc in normal way, 1dc front around each of next 5dc, rep from * to end, 1dc into top of turning chain. Turn.
4th row As 2nd.
5th row Ch 3, skip first dc, 1dc into each of next 5dc in normal way, *1dc front around each of next 5dc, 1dc into each of next 5dc in normal way, rep from * to end, 1dc into top of turning chain. Turn.
6th row Ch 3, skip first dc, 1dc into each of next 5dc in normal way, *1dc back around each of next 5dc, 1dc into each of next 5dc in normal way, rep from * to end, 1dc into top of turning chain. Turn.
7th row As 5th.
8th row As 6th.
9th row As 3rd.
10th row As 2nd.
The 3rd to 10th rows form pattern. Rep them throughout until the fabric is the depth you require.

Raised double crochet pattern

Here doubles worked around the stem are worked alternately with doubles

Basket weave variation

worked in the normal way to produce a highly textured, almost double fabric. The pattern is worked over an uneven number of stitches, and you should begin by making an uneven number of chains of any length.
1st row 1dc into 4th ch from hook, 1dc into each ch to end. Turn.
2nd row Ch 3, skip first dc, *1dc around stem of next dc inserting hook from right to left from the front to the back and around to the front of the work again — 1dc front — 1dc into top of next st in normal way, rep from * to end, 1dc into top of turning chain. Turn.

Raised double crochet pattern

3rd row Ch 3, skip first dc, 1dc into top of next dc in normal way, 1dc front around next dc, rep from * to last 2dc, 1dc into next dc, 1dc into top of turning chain. Turn.
4th row As 2nd row, but ending with 1dc front, 1dc into top of turning chain. Turn.
5th row As 3rd.
4th and 5th rows form pattern and are repeated throughout. Note that you alternate the doubles on each row by working 1dc front into the normal double worked in previous row and vice versa each time. Continue in this way to the required depth.

Tufted blanket

**Butterflies and flowers decorate this tufted blanket.
Worked in cotton, it is not only soft enough for a baby's skin
but is also hard wearing and easy to wash.**

Patterns and alternatives

Size
Completed blanket measures approximately 47in × 47in

Gauge
14 sts and 14 rows to 4in in extended sc (see below) worked on size E hook
To save time, check your gauge.

Materials
Approx 2,112yds of a medium-heavy cotton yarn
Size E crochet hook

Note: See Tufted patterns on page 162.

To make
Using size E hook, ch 152.
Base row (RS) Insert hook into 3rd ch from hook, yo and draw through a loop, yo and draw through first loop on hook, yo and draw through rem 2 loops on hook — extended sc or exsc formed —, 1exsc into each ch to end. Turn. 151 sts.

Next row Ch2 to count as first exsc, skip first st, 1exsc into each st to end. Turn.
Rep last row 10 times more.

Begin chart
Next row Ch2 to count as first exsc, skip first st, 1exsc into each of next 10 sts, *4exsc into next st, remove hook from loop and insert hook into first of 4exsc just worked, insert hook into loop just dropped and draw through first exsc — tuft formed —, 1exsc into each of next 31 sts, rep from * to last 12 sts, tuft into next st, 1exsc into each st to end. Turn.
Beg with a 2nd row, cont working from chart on page 117, ending with 117th row.
Next row (WS) Ch2 to count as first exsc, skip first st, 1exsc into each st to end. Turn.
Rep last row 10 times more.
Turn at end of last row.
Do not fasten off.

Border detail showing tufted flower motif

Edging
Next row Ch1, 2sc into first st, *1sc into each st to last st, 3sc into last st, 1sc into each row end to next corner, 3sc into first st on next edge*, rep from * to * once more, omitting 3sc at end of last rep, sl st to first ch.
Fasten off.
Lay blanket flat, pin it in shape and spray lightly with cold water.
Do not press, but allow to dry naturally away from direct heat.

Alternatives

Tufted patterns resemble candlewicking. Use them to add texture and interest to bedspreads and pillow covers.

Tufting is an easy way to add texture, design or pictures to a plain crochet fabric. For extra emphasis, you can work tufts in one or more contrasting colors. A number of picture, border and overall designs are suggested below. If you want something truly

Chart for blanket

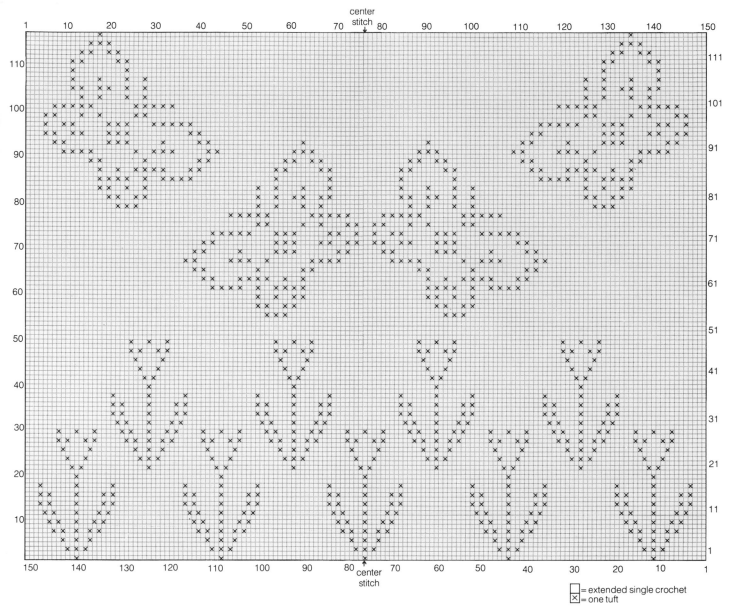

unique, create your own design. Before working out the design, make a gauge sample of extended single crochet (see Tufted patterns on page 162) in the yarn and hook you plan to use. Count the number of stitches and rows in four inches. You can then work out how many stitches and rows you will need to get the required size in the finished item.

Chart your design on graph paper with each square representing one stitch and mark the position of the tufts with a cross. Write the row numbers along the side and the stitch numbers along the top.

Tufted patterns can be worked in most smooth yarns. Thick cotton is especially effective because it forms a strong, crunchy fabric. And cotton yarn can usually be dyed before it is worked if you wish. Plain colors work best, but an overall pattern in a tweedy yarn can be effective.

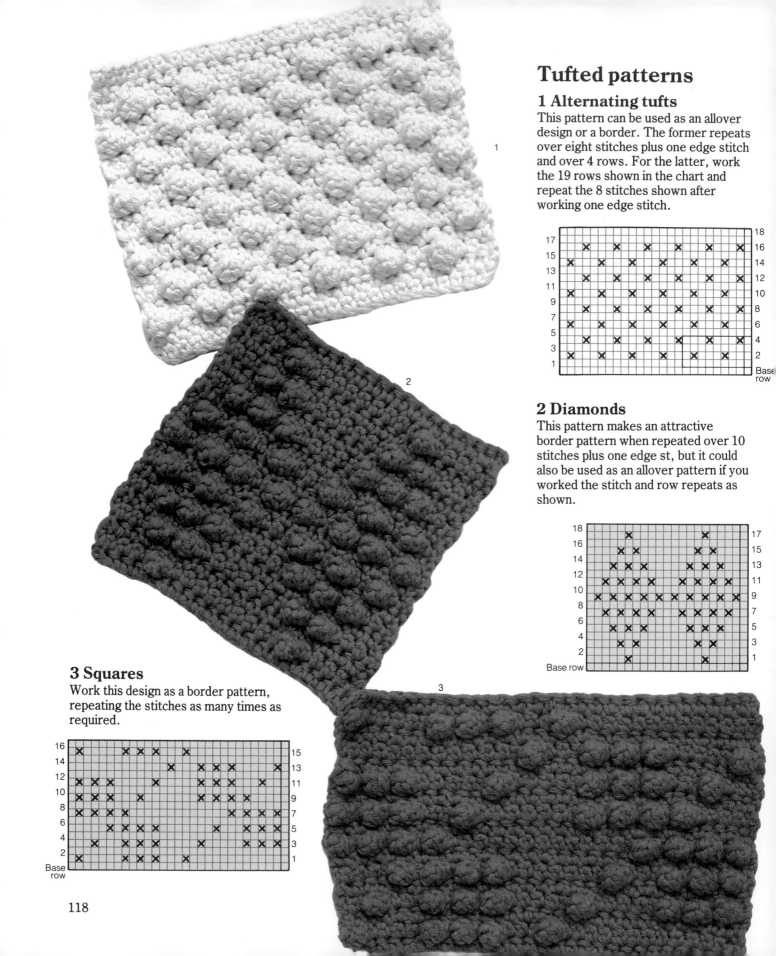

Tufted patterns

1 Alternating tufts

This pattern can be used as an allover design or a border. The former repeats over eight stitches plus one edge stitch and over 4 rows. For the latter, work the 19 rows shown in the chart and repeat the 8 stitches shown after working one edge stitch.

2 Diamonds

This pattern makes an attractive border pattern when repeated over 10 stitches plus one edge st, but it could also be used as an allover pattern if you worked the stitch and row repeats as shown.

3 Squares

Work this design as a border pattern, repeating the stitches as many times as required.

4 Star

This pattern should be used as an all-over design. Work the base row, repeating the 18 stitches and 18 rows as required.

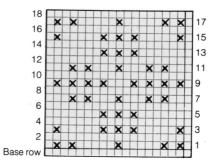

5 Zigzag

For a border pattern, work one edge stitch then repeat the 22 stitches as shown in the chart. For an allover pattern, repeat over 22 stitches and 20 rows after working the edge stitch and base row respectively.

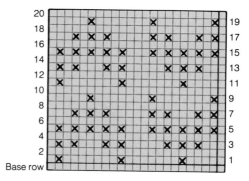

6 Bow

Repeat the 25 stitches of the chart if you are working this design as a border pattern. For an allover pattern, repeat the 25 stitches and 20 rows of the chart.

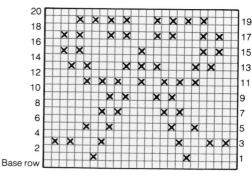

Finishing touches

Braid trim

We've used fine cotton and feather-stitch braid to decorate an antique sewing table. It's one of many useful braid patterns.

Patterns and alternatives

Sizes
Each braid measures approx ⅜in wide

Materials
For Chain, Traditional feather-stitch and Picot braids:
A size 5 crochet cotton
For Two-color twisted braid:
A size 5 crochet cotton
Metallic Knit-cro-sheen
For Beaded braid:
A size 5 crochet cotton
Small round beads (approx 6 beads to 4in of braid)
For Two-color looped braid:
A size 5 crochet cotton in two colors, (A) and (B)
Size O steel crochet hook

Note: It takes about 47yds of size 5 crochet cotton to make 1yd of braid.

Note: See Working in fine cotton on page 14.

Traditional feather-stitch braid
Using size O steel hook, ch7, sl st into first ch to form a circle.
1st row Ch 3, 3dc into circle, ch3, 1sc into circle. Turn.
2nd row Ch 3, 3dc into 3ch sp, ch3, 1sc into same sp. Turn.
2nd row forms pat. Rep for length required and fasten off.

Chain braid
Using size O steel hook, ch4.
Base 1tr into 4th ch from hook, turn, *ch4, 1tr into sp between tr and ch, turn, rep from * for length required.

Do not fasten off.
1st row Working into one edge of base, *2sc into sp between tr and ch, ch3, rep from * to end, ending with 2sc. Fasten off.
2nd row Work as 1st row, working into other edge of base.
Fasten off.

Beaded braid
Before beginning, thread beads onto yarn as required.
Ch12.
Base row 1sc into 10th ch from hook, 1sc into next ch, 1sc into last ch. turn.
1st row Ch 3, sl st to top of 1st sc, ch5, 3sc into 9ch loop. Turn.
2nd row Ch 3, sl st to top of 1st sc, ch5, 3sc into 5ch loop. Turn.
2nd row forms pat. Rep for length required, but on every 4th row, after working 5ch and before working 3sc, slide bead up to hook, so that it is incorporated into the work.

Two-color looped braid
Using size O steel hook and A, ch6.
Base 1dc into 5th ch from hook, 1sc into last ch, turn, *ch4, 1dc into sc, 1sc into dc, rep from * for length required. Fasten off.
1st row Using B and working into one edge of base, 1sc into first sc, *ch5, 1sc into side of next sc, rep from * to end.
Fasten off.
2nd row Work as 1st row working into other edge of base.
Fasten off.

Two-color twisted braid
Base Using size 5 crochet cotton, work as for base of Chain braid. Fasten off.
1st row Using metallic Knit-cro-sheen and working into one edge of base, sl st into first sp at end of base, *ch4, remove hook from loop, insert into next sp on base and pick up dropped loop, rep from * to end. Fasten off.
2nd row Work as 1st row, working into other edge of base. Fasten off.

Picot braid
Base Work as base of Chain braid. Do not fasten off.
1st row Working into one edge of base, (2sc, ch3, 2sc) into first sp at end of braid, *(2sc, ch3, 2sc) into next sp, rep from * to end. Fasten off.
2nd row Work as 1st row, working into other edge of base.
Fasten off.

Alternatives

Use our braids to decorate everything from lampshades and fabric-covered picture frames to upholstered chair seats.

Versatile braid in simple or elaborate patterns and in one or many colors can be used singly or mixed to decorate hundreds of accessories around the house. Consider what braid could do for café curtains or shades, for example, or a fabric sewing box.
Sew braid to woven fabrics with small, neat stitches in a strong sewing thread

that matches the braid. Braid that is colorfast can be washed along with the item it trims. If you are uncertain whether it is colorfast, attach a small piece of the braid to a piece of white cloth and wash as you would the item. Check to see if the color has run. When you attach braid to an item that cannot be washed such as a lampshade or a wooden chair frame, use fabric or wood glue.

Beads and ribbon can make braid look extra special, but they must be able to take the same treatment you intend to give the braid. And like braids, they too should be colorfast.

Braids are best worked with a steel hook and fine cotton or synthetic thread. A numbers 3 or 5 thread produces a neat, firm appearance and is suitable for most braids. Threads with a high twist and luster are

especially effective. When beads are incorporated, they should be small so they do not distort the braid. They should not be used on chair seats.

Special technique — working braids

1 *Braids are not worked lengthwise on a long foundation chain, but widthwise on a very small number of chains. This avoids complicated calculations about the number of chains to make. Simply work the braid for the length required and fasten off.*

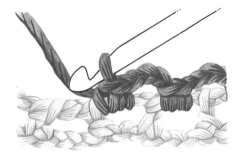

2 *Some braids are completed by working into the long edges of the base, sometimes in one or two contrasting colors. The illustration above shows one edge of Chain braid being worked in a second color.*

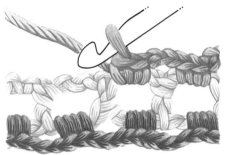

3 *The appearance of the braid can be varied by using a third color, as above. You can also use the same color you used on the first edge or work the entire braid in a single color.*

Special technique — working with beads

1 *To thread beads onto yarn use a fine sewing needle and sewing thread. Thread the needle and tie the two ends together. Loop the yarn to be used over the thread loop and then use the needle and thread to slip the beads onto the yarn.*

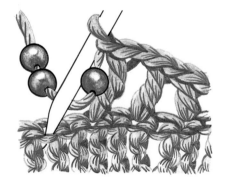

2 *Keep the beads at the front of the fabric when working a bead stitch. Push the bead up close to the hook and insert the hook into the correct stitch so that the yarn is held behind the bead.*

3 *Hook the yarn behind the bead and draw the loop of yarn through the stitch. Complete the stitch holding the bead at the front of the work so that the bead will remain in place once the stitch has been completed.*

Patterns and alternatives

1 Puff lace braid

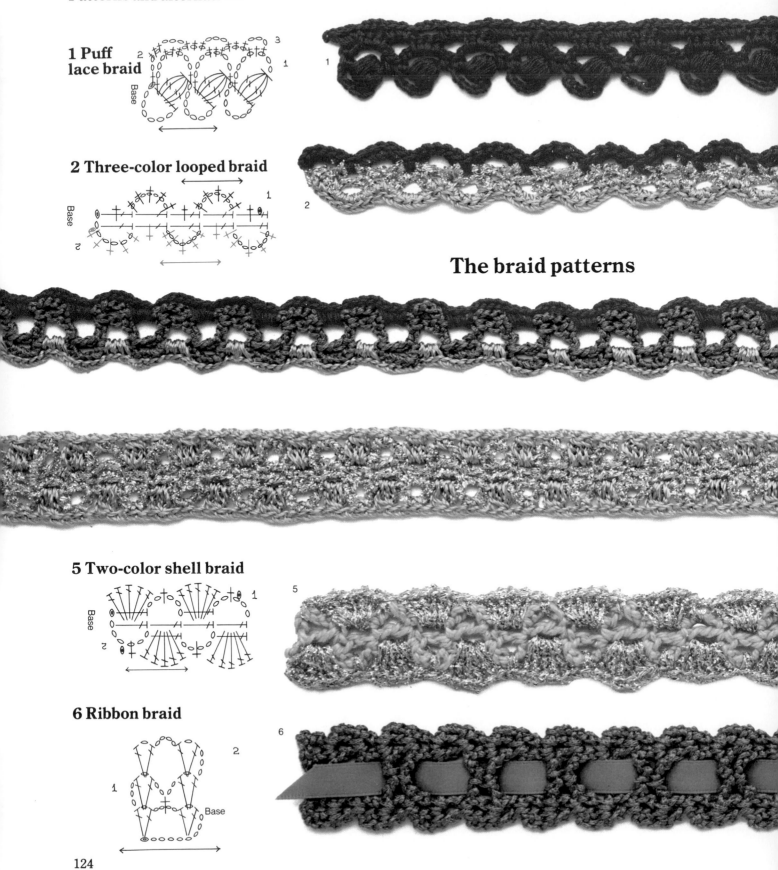

2 Three-color looped braid

The braid patterns

5 Two-color shell braid

6 Ribbon braid

124

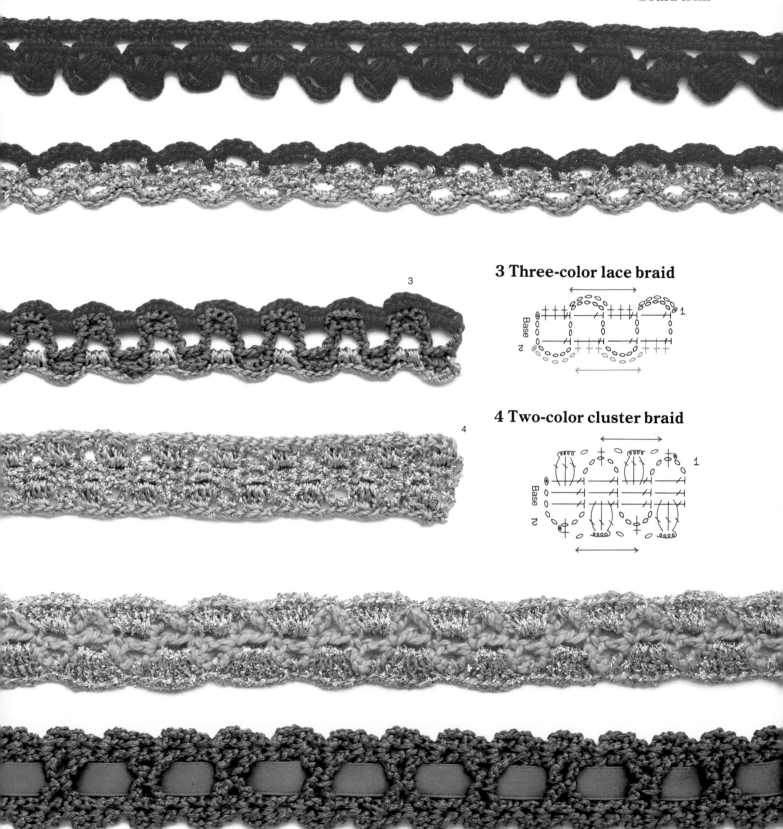

3 Three-color lace braid

4 Two-color cluster braid

Venetian lampshade

Shed new light on Irish crochet by working Venetian motifs
in fine cotton and using them to trim a plain lampshade.
Or add extra style with a pretty edging.

Size
Arranged motifs measure
approximately 9in square

Gauge
Flower measures approximately 2in
between widest points
To save time, check your gauge.

Materials
354yds of a size 20 crochet cotton
make motifs shown and 2 edgings
Size 8 steel crochet hook
Unless otherwise stated, all cords are
formed from 8 strands of size 20
crochet cotton.

Note: See Working in fine cotton on
page 14.

Flower (make 6)
Using size 8 steel hook, ch5, sl st to
first ch to form a circle.
1st round Ch2, 11sc into circle, sl st
to top of first 2ch.
2nd round Ch2, 2sc into first sc, (1sc
into next sc, 2sc into next sc) 5 times,
sl st to top of first 2ch. 18 sts.
Petals *Ch8, sl st to first of 8ch to
form a circle, (1sc, 1hdc, 6dc, 3tr, 6dc,
1hdc, 1sc) into circle, sl st into each of
next 3sc of 2nd round, rep from * 5
times more.
Fasten off.

Tulip (make 2)
Using size 8 steel hook, ch30.
Base row Working over cord
throughout, 1sc into 2nd ch from hook,
1sc into each ch to end. Turn. 29sc.
1st row Ch1, 1sc into each of first
16sc, work 18sc over cord only. Turn.
2nd row Ch1, 1sc into each of first
15sc, (skip next sc, 1sc into next sc) 4
times, 1sc into next sc, work 12sc over
cord only. Turn.

3rd row Ch1, 1sc into each of first
11sc, (skip next sc, 1sc into next sc) 4
times, 1sc into next sc, work 12sc over
cord only. Turn.
4th row Ch1, 1sc into each of first
11sc, (skip next sc, 1sc into next sc) 3
times, 1sc into next sc, work 12sc over
cord only. Turn.
5th row Ch1, 1sc into each of first
14sc.
Fasten off.

Scroll (make 2)
Using size 8 steel hook, work 60sc
over cord, *twist last 20sc worked to
form a circle, sl st to first of these 20sc,
sl st into 2nd sc of circle.*
* * Working over cord only, work 36sc,
rep from * to *.
Work from * * 3 times more.
Fasten off.

Floret (make 4)
Using size 8 steel hook, ch6, sl st to
first ch to form a circle.
1st round Ch 1, working over cord
work 24sc into circle, sl st to first sc.
Break off cord.
2nd round *Sl st into next sc, 1hdc
into next sc, 3dc into next sc, 1hdc into
next sc, rep from * to end, sl st into
first sl st.
Fasten off.

Leaves and stem (make 1)
Stem Using size 8 steel hook, ch 60.
1st row Working over cord work 1sc
into 3rd ch from hook, 1sc into each ch
to end. Fasten off.
Leaf Using size 8 steel hook, ch14.
1st row Working over cord
throughout work 1sc into 3rd ch from
hook, 1sc into each ch to last ch, 3sc
into last ch, 1sc into each ch along
other side of leaf, sl st into position on
stem. Fasten off.

Make 6 more leaves and attach to stem
with a sl st, spacing leaves evenly.

Edging (make 2)
Using size 8 steel hook, make
foundation ch approximately 4in longer
than the circumference of the top of the
lampshade.
1st row Ch 1, working over cord work
1sc into each ch until length of crochet
is same as circumference of top of
lampshade and the number of sc is a
multiple of 8 plus 7.
2nd row Ch 4, *skip next sc, 1dc into
next sc, rep from * to end. Turn.
3rd row Ch 1, 1sc into first ch sp,
*ch10, sl st into 7th ch from hook to
form a circle, (1sc, 12dc, 1sc) into
circles, ch3, skip next ch sp, 1sc into
next ch sp, (1sc into next dc, 1sc into
next ch sp) twice, rep from * to end
omitting 3sc at end of last rep.
Fasten off. Undo excess ch and darn in
loose ends.
Make another edging in the same way
to fit circumference of lower edge of
lampshade.

To finish
Using stab stitch (see page 154) and
matching yarn, sew edgings to top and
lower edges of lampshade (lower
edging should extend below rim of
lampshade).
Using pins or sticky tape, attach motifs
to lampshade in arrangement shown on
page 127 or as required. Using stab
stitch and matching yarn, sew motifs to
lampshade.
Remove pins or tape.

Alternatives

Scrolls, flowers, leaves and stems characteristic of Venetian gros point lace can be made in single crochet and used to decorate household accessories.

To create your own lampshade design, make a sketch using some of the motifs on the lampshade or below. Make the motifs and pin them to the sketch. Then glue (with fabric to fabric glue) or sew them (see Stab stitch on page 154) to the shade one by one. You can also sew the motifs to a fabric such as linen to decorate a tablecloth or a pillow cover. Or cover a jewelry box with fabric and decorate it with Venetian motifs. You can also sew the motifs to a picot mesh for a lacy bedspread. See Irish crochet on page 160.
Venetian motifs look best when worked in fine cotton. Any thickness from a size 5 to a size 60 is suitable for the motifs — the thicker the thread, the larger the motif. Pressing flattens the texture; instead pin the motifs into shape, spray lightly with water and allow them to dry naturally away from direct heat.

Special technique — working Venetian scrolls

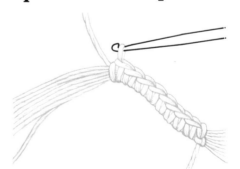

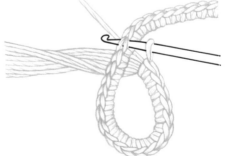

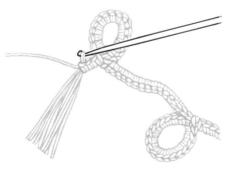

1 *Scrolls are especially characteristic of Venetian crochet and can be made easily in single crochet. Make a cord about 10in in length by twisting together eight strands of crochet cotton in a color matching the working yarn. Using the working yarn and a fine crochet hook, work 60 single crochet over the cord.*

2 *Twist the last 20 single crochet as shown to form a circle. Work a slip stitch into the first of these 20 single crochet stitches to anchor the circle. Slip stitch into the second stitch on the circle.*

3 *Work a further 36 single crochet over the cord only and repeat step 2. Continue in this way to the other end of the cord or for the number of twists required, twisting to the right or wrong side as you wish. Fasten off and trim the cord close to the stitches.*

Venetian motifs

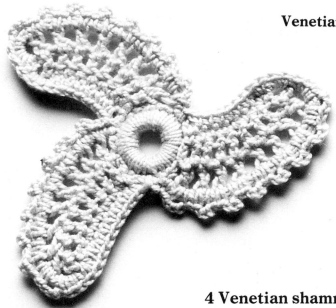

1 Triple leaf

Wind yarn 16 times around index finger to form a circle.

1st round Work 21sc into circle, sl st to first sc.

2nd round * * Ch 20, 1dc into 6th ch from hook, *ch1, skip next ch, 1dc into next ch, rep from * 6 times more, ch1, skip next 2sc, sl st into next sc. Turn.

Next row Sl st into each of next 6sc, 1dc into base of next 9dc. Turn.

Next row Ch1, 1sc into each st to center circle, 1 sl st into each of next 4sc on circle. * *

Rep from * * to * * twice more.

Next round * * * Working over cord formed from 8 strands of crochet cotton, work *1 sc into each 1ch sp, 1sc into next dc, ch3, rep from * 8 times more, 5sc into tip of leaf, 8sc down 2nd side, sl st to center of 3 sl st on ring, rep from * * * to end. Fasten off.

3 Venetian rose

Wind yarn 20 times around index finger to form a circle.

1st round Work 20sc into circle, sl st to first sc.

2nd round 1sc into same place as sl st, * ch4, skip next 3sc, 1sc into next sc, rep from * ending with sl st into first sc.

3rd round Working over cord formed from 8 strands of crochet cotton, work (1 sl st, 10sc, 1 sl st) into each 4ch loop.

4th round *Ch 6, 1sc around next sc on 2nd round, rep from * to end.

5th round Working over cord, work (1 sl st, 15sc, 1 sl st) into each 6ch loop.

6th round As 4th round, making 8ch between sl st.

7th round As 5th, working 20sc between each sl st. Fasten off.

4 Venetian shamrock

Wind yarn 20 times around index finger to form a circle.

1st round (12sc, ch10) 3 times into circle, sl st to first sc. Turn.

2nd round Working over a cord formed from 8 strands of crochet cotton, * work 28sc into 10ch loop, skip next 4sc, 1sc into each of next 2sc, ch3, 1sc into each of next 2sc, rep from * twice more, ending with sl st into first of first 30sc.

3rd round * (Ch 4, 1sc into each of next 3sc) 9 times, sl st into next 3ch loop, 1sc into first of next 30sc, rep from * ending with sl st into next 3ch loop, sl st into next sc.

Stem Working over cord only work 30sc. Turn.

1st row Ch 1, 1sc into each sc to end, sl st to base of shamrock. Fasten off.

2 Star

Wind yarn 20 times around index finger to form a circle.

1st round Work 30sc into circle, sl st to first sc.

2nd round 1sc into same place as sl st, *ch5, sl st into 3rd of 5ch, ch2, skip next 4sc, 1sc into sc, rep from * ending with sl st into first sc. Fasten off.

Patterns and alternatives

7 Open flower
Wind yarn 20 times around index finger to form a circle.
1st round Work 24sc into circle, sl st to first sc.
2nd round 1sc into same place as sl st, *ch9, skip next 2sc, 1sc into next sc, rep from * ending with sl st into first sc.
3rd round *15sc into next 9ch loop, rep from * to end, sl st into first sc. Fasten off.

6 Acorn
Wind yarn 16 times around index finger to form a circle.
1st round Work 24sc into circle, sl st to first sc.
2nd round Ch 1, 1sc into each of first 6sc, ch3, skip next sc, 1dc into next sc, ch4, skip next 3sc, 1dtr into next sc, ch2, inserting hook behind dtr just worked work 1dtr into 2nd of 3sc just skipped, ch4, skip sc after first dtr, 1dc into next sc, ch3, skip next sc, 1sc into each of next 9sc, sl st to first sc.
3rd round Ch 1, working over cord formed from 8 strands of crochet cotton, work 1sc into each of next 6sc, (2sc, ch3) 3 times into next 3ch sp, 3 times into next 4ch sp, twice into next 2ch sp, 3 times into next 4ch sp and 3 times into last 3ch sp, 1sc into each sc to end, sl st into first sc. Fasten off.

5 Leaf
Ch 32.
1st row Working over cord formed from 8 strands of crochet cotton, work 1sc into 3rd ch from hook, 1sc into each of next 29sc, working into other side of foundation ch, work 3sc into first sc, 1sc into each of next 14sc. Turn.
2nd row Ch 1, 1sc into each of first 16sc, 3sc into next sc at tip of leaf, 1sc into each of next 14sc. Turn.
3rd row Ch 1, 1sc into each of next 16sc, 3sc into next sc, 1sc into each of next 16sc, 1sc into each of next 2 row ends, sl st to stem. Turn.
4th row Ch 1, (1sc into each of next 2sc, ch3, 1sc into same sc as last sc, 1sc into each of next 2sc) 9 times, 1sc into each of next 2 row ends, 1sc into each sc of stem to end. Fasten off.

8 Pineapple
Ch4, sl st to first ch to form a circle.
1st row Ch 4, 8tr into circle. Turn.
2nd row *Ch 4, 1sc into sp between next 2tr, rep from * to last sp. Turn. 8 loops.
3rd row Sl st to 2nd of first 4ch, *ch4, 1sc into next 4ch loop, rep from * to end. Turn. 7 loops.
Rep last row, working one fewer loop on each row, until there is one loop only. Fasten off.
Next row Rejoin yarn to base of motif, inserting hook into 4ch circle, working over cord formed from 8 strands of crochet cotton, work 1sc into 4ch circle, 3sc into next tr, (2sc, ch3, 2sc) into each row end to within point of motif, (2sc, ch3, 2sc, ch3, 2sc) into 3ch loop at point of motif, (2sc, ch3, 2sc) into each row end to first row of motif, 2sc into next tr, 1sc into 4ch circle, sl st to first sc. Fasten off.

Shelf edging

The pattern for the deep edging is given here. For the narrower one work in exactly the same way but omit rows 2, 3 and 4.

Size

To fit along edge of shelves as required (shelves here were each 28¼in long)

Gauge

2¾in at widest point
To save time, check your gauge.

Materials

A size 20 crochet cotton. (The edgings shown here used 354yds)
Size 7 steel crochet hook

Deep scalloped edging

Make a crochet cord (see page 160) as required, having a multiple of 16 loops plus 7 along one edge.
1st row Sl st into first loop, ch3, skip 2 loops, (2dc, ch2, 2dc) into next loop, *skip 3 loops, (2dc, ch2, 2dc) into next loop, rep from * to last 3 loops, skip 2 loops, 1dc into last loop. Turn.
2nd row Ch 3, (2dc, ch2, 2dc) into each 2ch sp to end, 1dc into top of turning ch. Turn.

3rd and 4th rows As 2nd row.
5th row Ch 3, *(2dc, ch2, 2dc) into next 2ch sp, ch2, 1sc into next 2ch sp, 7dc into next 2ch sp, 1sc into next sp, ch2, rep from * ending (2dc, ch2, 2dc) into last 2ch sp, 1dc into top of turning ch. Turn.
6th row Ch 3, (2dc, ch2, 2dc) into first 2 ch sp, *(ch1, 1dc into next dc) 7 times, ch1, (2dc, ch2, 2dc) into next 2ch, rep from *, ending 1dc into top of turning ch. Turn.
7th row Ch 3, (2dc, ch2, 2dc) into first 2ch sp, *(ch3, 1sc into next 1 ch sp) 6 times, ch3, (2dc, ch2, 2dc) into next 2ch sp, rep from *, ending 1dc into top of turning ch. Turn.
8th row Ch 3, (2dc, ch2, 2dc) into first 2ch sp, *ch3, skip next 3ch sp, (1sc into next 3ch sp, skip next 3ch sp, ch3) 5 times, (2dc; ch2, 2dc) into 2ch sp, rep from *, ending 1dc into top of turning ch. Turn.
9th row Ch 3, (2dc, ch2, 2dc, ch2, 2dc) into first 2ch sp, *ch3, skip next

3ch sp, (1sc into next 3ch sp, ch3) 4 times, (2dc, ch2, 2dc, ch2, 2dc) into next 2ch sp, rep from *, ending 1dc into top of turning ch. Turn.
10th row Sl st over first (2dc, ch2, 2dc) and into next 2ch sp, ch3, (1dc, ch2, 2dc) into same sp, ch3, skip next 3ch sp, (1sc into next 3ch sp, ch3) 3 times, (2dc, ch2, 2dc) into next 2ch sp. Turn and complete this leaf separately.
11th row Sl st into 2ch sp, ch3, (1dc, ch2, 2dc) into same sp, ch3, skip next 3ch sp, (1sc into 3ch sp, ch3) twice, (2dc, ch2, 2dc) into next 2ch sp. Turn.
12th row Sl st into 2ch sp, ch3, (1dc, ch2, 2dc) into same sp, ch3, skip next 3ch sp, 1sc into 3ch sp, ch3, (2dc, ch2, 2dc) into next 2ch sp. Turn.
13th row Sl st into 2ch sp, ch3, leaving the last loop of each double on hook, work 3dc, into same place as sl st, yo, draw through all 4 loops on hook, sl st to next 2ch sp. Fasten off. Rejoin yarn to first 2ch sp of next leaf; finish as for first leaf. Rep to end.

Wired flowers

Preserve the freshness of springtime by working these flowers and displaying them in twos or threes or in large bunches.

Sizes

One tulip petal measures approx 2½in in height
One daffodil petal measures approx 1½in in height
One small iris petal measures approx 2in in height

Gauge

12 sts to 1¼in over dc using size 8 steel crochet hook
To save time, check your gauge.

Materials

A size 20 crochet cotton, in small amounts of each of the foll colors:
Tulip Pink and green
Daffodil Yellow and gold
Iris Purple, gold and green
Large leaves Green
Size 8 steel crochet hook
Fine, soft craft wire for flowers
Florist's thick wire in lengths required for stems
Florist's green tape
Artificial stamens to suit flower

Note: When wiring flowers, see page 138.

Tulip

Petals (make 6)

Using size 8 steel hook and pink, ch5.
Base row (RS) 2dc into 4th ch from hook, 3dc into last ch. Turn. 6 sts.
1st row Ch 3, 1dc into dc at base of first 3ch, 2dc into next dc, 1dc into each of next 2dc, 2dc into each of last 2 sts. Turn. 10 sts.
2nd and 3rd rows As 1st row. 18 sts.
4th row Ch 3, skip first st, 1dc into each st to end. Turn.
5th – 8th rows As 4th row.
9th row Ch 3, skip first st, (work next 2dc tog) 8 times, 1dc into last st. Turn.

10 sts.
10th row Ch 1 to count as first sc, skip first st, 1sc into next dc, 1dc into each of next 6dc, 1sc into next dc. Fasten off.
Cut a piece of craft wire to fit all around petal plus approx 4in. Arrange wire around petal so that 2 lengths, each approx 2in, extend below base of petal. With RS facing, rejoin pink to base of petal and, covering wire at the same time, work a row of sc into all edges of petal, working 1sc into each st and 2sc into each dc row end. Fasten off.

Leaf (make 1)

Using size 8 steel hook and green, ch50.

Base row (WS) 1dc into 4th ch from hook, 1dc into each ch to last ch, 5dc into last ch, working into other edge of chain, 1dc into each ch to first 4ch. Turn.
Next row Ch 1, *1sc into each of next 10 sts, 1hdc into each of next 8 sts, 1dc into each of next 10 sts, 1tr into each of next 10 sts, 1dc into each of next 4 sts, 1hdc into each of next 4 sts, 1sc into each st to 3rd of 5dc at end of leaf, 3sc into 3rd dc, now work in reverse ending at *, ending at base of Leaf. Fasten off.
Wire Leaf as for Tulip petal, working 1sc into each st.

To finish

Holding stamens in the center, overlap petals to form Tulip and tape onto thick wire to form stem. Tape Leaf into position and then tape rest of stem.

Daffodil

Note: See Working into a single loop on page 149.

Trumpet

Using size 8 steel hook and gold, ch4, sl st to first ch to form a circle.
1st round Ch 3, 9dc into circle, sl st to top of first 3ch. 10 sts.
2nd round Ch 2, skip first st, 1sc into each st to end, sl st to top of first 2ch.
3rd round Ch 3, skip first st, *2dc into next st, 1dc into each of next 2 sts, rep from * twice more, sl st to top of first 3ch. 13 sts.
4th round As 2nd round.
5th round Working into front loops only of each st, ch3, skip first st, 2dc into each st to end, sl st to top of first 3ch. 25 sts.
6th round As 2nd round.
7th round Ch 3, skip first st, 1dc into

each dc, sl st to top of first 3ch.

8th – 11th rounds Rep 6th and 7th rounds twice more.

12th round As 6th round.

13th round Ch 3, skip first st, 2dc into each st to end. 49 sts.

14th round Ch 1, 1hdc into same place as 1ch, *3dc into next st, (1hdc, 1sc) into next st, (1sc, 1hdc) into next st, rep from * to end.
Fasten off.

Petals (make 6)

Using size 8 steel hook, join yellow to free loop of first st on 5th round of Trumpet.

* *1st row** Working into free loops of 5th round, ch3, 1dc into same place as 3ch, 2dc into next st, 2dc into next st. Turn. 6 sts.

2nd row Ch 3, skip first st, 2dc into each of next 4dc, 1dc into last st. Turn. 10 sts.

3rd row Ch 3, skip first st, 2dc into next dc, 1dc into each of next 6dc, 2dc into next dc, 1dc into last st. Turn. 12 sts.

4th row Ch 3, skip first st, 1dc into each st to end. Turn.

5th and 6th rows As 4th row.

7th row Ch 3, skip first st, *work next 2dc tog, rep from * 4 times more, 1dc into last st. Turn. 8 sts.

8th row Ch 3, skip first st, *work next

2dc tog, rep from * twice more, 1dc into last st.

9th row Ch 3, skip first st, work next 3dc tog, 1dc into last st.
Fasten off. * *

Using size 8 steel hook, join yellow to same loop as last 2dc worked on first row of previous petal.
Rep from * * to * *.

Work 4 more petals in this way. Cut a piece of craft wire to fit all around petals plus approx 4in. Arrange wire around petals so that 2 lengths, each approx 2in, extend below base of one petal.

Working over wire, edge petals with sc as for Tulip petals.
Fasten off.

To finish

Twist petal wire around thick wire to form stem. Bind stem and petal wire with tape.

Iris

Two-color petal (make 3)

Using size 8 steel hook and gold, ch20.

Base row Working over wire throughout, work 1sc into 2nd ch from hook, 1sc into each of next 10ch, 1hdc

into each of next 6ch, 2dc into next ch, (3dc, 1tr, 3dc) into last ch, working into other side of ch, work 2dc into next ch, 1hdc into each of next 6ch, 1sc into each ch to end. Turn.
Break off gold and wire leaving 2 ends of wire, each 2in, at base of petal. Join in purple.

Next row *Ch 1, 1sc into each of first 3 sts, 1hdc into each of next 6 sts, 1dc into each of next 7 sts, 1tr into next st* *, 2tr into each of next 10 sts, 1tr into next st, 1 tr into each of next 7 sts, 1hdc into each of next 6 sts, 1sc into each st to end. Fasten off.

Large purple petal (make 3)

Using size 8 steel hook and purple, ch20.
Using purple, wire and work base row as for Two-color petal.

Next row Using purple, work from * to * * as for Two-color petal, 2tr into each of next 2 sts, (1tr, 1dtr) into next st, 2dtr into next st, (1dtr, 1tr tr) into next st, ch5, sl st into same st, sl st into next st, ch5, (1tr tr, 1dtr) into same st, 2dtr into next st, (1dtr, 1tr) into next st, 2tr into each of next 2 sts, now work from * * to * in reverse.
Fasten off.

Small purple petal (make 3)

Using size 8 steel hook and purple, work ch, and wire and work base row as for Two-color petal. Fasten off.

Leaf (make 2)

Using size 8 steel hook and green, ch30.

Base row 1sc into 2nd ch from hook, 1sc into each of next 5ch, 1hdc into each of next 5ch, 1dc into each of next 17ch, 5dc into last ch, working into other edge of foundation ch, work 1dc into each of next 17ch, 1hdc into each of next 5ch, 1sc into each ch to end. Turn.
Wire and edge Leaf as for Tulip leaf.

To finish

Place petals together as shown opposite, bending petals as required. Tape flower wires to thick wire to form stem and tape to position of leaf. Bind leaf to stem and tape rem stem.

Large leaves

Using size 8 steel hook and green, ch80.

Base row Working over craft wire throughout, work 1dc into 4th ch from hook, 1dc into each ch to last ch, 5dc into last ch, working into other side of ch work 1dc into each ch to last 3ch. Turn. Cut wire, leaving 2in ends.

Next row Ch 1 to count as first sc, skip first st, 1sc into each of next 50 sts, 1hdc into each of next 10 sts, 1dc into each of next 16 sts, 1hdc into each of next 2 sts, 1sc into next st, 3 sl st into st at tip of leaf, 1sc into next st, 1hdc into each of next 2 sts, 1dc into each of next 16 sts, 1hdc into each of next 10 sts, 1sc into each of next 10 sts, sl st into next dc, turn.

Next row 1sc into each of next 5 sts, 1hdc into each of next 10 sts, 1dc into each of next 20 sts, 1hdc into each of next 3 sts, 1sc into each of next 2 sts, 3sc into st at tip of leaf, 1sc into each of next 2 sts, 1hdc into each of next 3 sts, 1dc into each of next 20 sts, 1hdc into each of next 10 sts, 1sc into each of next 10 sts, sl st into next st, turn.

Next row 1sc into each of next 5 sts, 1hdc into each of next 10 sts, 1dc into each of next 26 sts, 1hdc into each of next 3 sts, 1sc into each of next 2 sts, 3sc into st at tip of leaf, 1sc into each of

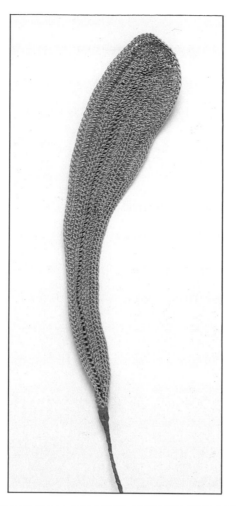

next 2 sts, 1hdc into each of next 3 sts, 1dc into each of next 26 sts, 1hdc into each of next 10 sts, 1sc into each st to end. Turn.

Next row Working over craft wire, work a row of sc all around leaf. Fasten off.

Tape leaf onto wire as required.

Alternatives

Add variety to your bouquet with a wider range of flowers and colors. Both the Tulip and the Iris could be worked in other colors, for example. And by using a golden orange for the Daffodil trumpet and white for the petals, you could create a Narcissus.

Working green plants

Realistic green plants can also be crocheted. For those with small leaves, like *Adiantum*, use a size 20 cotton thread. Work larger-leafed plants like *Philodendron* in a size 5 cotton. Thick stems can be made from narrow single-crochet tubes, wired with florist's thick wire. Use bouclé yarn to represent soil and work the pot in plain brown yarn or use a real pot.

To avoid crochet plants tipping over, weight the bottom of the pot with sand.

Special technique — large, separate leaves

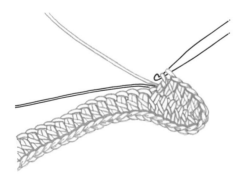

1 *A few large leaves add realism to a flower arrangement. Those on page 133 are worked in much the same way as the flowers. Chain 80 and work the base row over thin craft wire, leaving two 2in-long ends extending from the leaf base.*

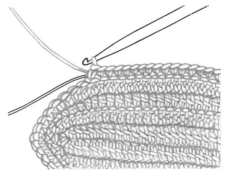

2 *Work the next three rows as instructed in the pattern. Cut a piece of thin craft wire to fit all around the leaf plus approximately 4in. Work a row of sc into the edges of the leaf, at the same time working over the wire so that two 2in-long ends extend from the lower edge.*

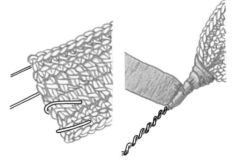

3 *If you are using a short vase, cut off about 1½in from each wire and bend back the remainder to secure (above left). To make a stem, twist the leaf wires around a length of thick wire cut to the length required. Bind the leaf to the stem with green tape (above right).*

Patterns and alternatives

Wired flower patterns

1 Freesia

Using random cotton, ch4, sl st to first ch to form a circle.

1st round Ch 3, working over approx 6in of wire, work 8dc into circle, sl st to top of first 3ch. 9 sts.

2nd round Ch 3, skip first st, 1dc into each st to end, sl st to top of first 3ch.

3rd round Ch 3, skip first st, 2dc into next st, (1dc into each of next 2 sts, 2dc into next st) twice, 1dc into next st, sl st to top of first 3ch. 12 sts.

4th round Ch 3, skip first st, (2dc into next st, 1dc into each of next 2 sts) 3 times, 2dc into next st, 1dc into next st, sl st to top of first 3ch. 16 sts.

5th round Ch 3, skip first st, (2dc into next st, 1dc into next st) 7 times, 2dc into last st, sl st to top of first 3ch. 24 sts.

6th round As 2nd round.

7th round Ch 3, 1dc into base of 3ch, (3tr into next st, 2dc into next st, sl st into next st, 2dc into next st) 5 times, 3tr into next st, 2dc into next st, sl st into next st.

Fasten off.

Make 3 more flowers in the same way. Cut length of thick wire and bend over for approx ½in at one end. Bind with

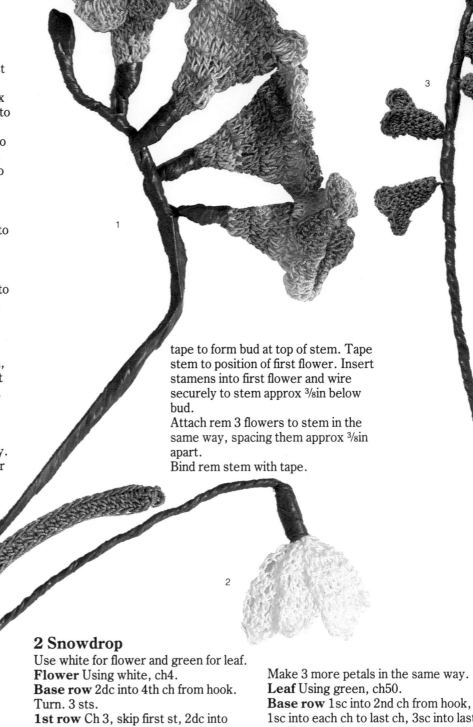

tape to form bud at top of stem. Tape stem to position of first flower. Insert stamens into first flower and wire securely to stem approx ⅜in below bud.

Attach rem 3 flowers to stem in the same way, spacing them approx ⅜in apart.

Bind rem stem with tape.

2 Snowdrop

Use white for flower and green for leaf.

Flower Using white, ch4.

Base row 2dc into 4th ch from hook. Turn. 3 sts.

1st row Ch 3, skip first st, 2dc into each of next 2 sts. Turn. 5 sts.

2nd and 3rd rows Ch 3, skip first st, 1dc into each st to end. Turn.

4th row Ch 3, skip first st, work next 4dc tog.

Fasten off.

Make 3 more petals in the same way.

Leaf Using green, ch50.

Base row 1sc into 2nd ch from hook, 1sc into each ch to last ch, 3sc into last ch. Turn.

Next row Working over craft wire, work 1sc into each ch on other side of foundation to end.

Fasten off. Cut craft wire, leaving a 2in-long end.

Place 4 petals together as shown. Bind lower edges of petals tog with tape. Bind and attach flower to stem. Bind stem to position of leaf. Attach leaf to stem and bind rem stem.

3 Bluebell

Bud Using blue, ch6 leaving a 2½in-long end of yarn.

Base row 1sc into 2nd ch from hook, 1dc into each of next 3ch, 1sc into last ch. Turn.

1st – 4th rows Ch 1, 1sc into first sc, 1dc into each of next 3dc, 1sc into last sc. Turn.

Fasten off, leaving a 2½in-long end of yarn.

Roll work into a tight bud over end of thick wire. Bind tape around bottom of bud and around ends and onto wire to form stem.

Flowers Using blue, ch4, sl st to first ch to form a circle. Leave a 2½in-long end of yarn.

1st round Ch 1, 8sc into circle, sl st to first sc. 9 sts.

2nd – 4th rounds Ch 1, 1sc into each sc to end, sl st to first sc.

5th round Ch 1, 2sc into each sc to end, sl st to first sc. 16 sts.

6th round Ch 1, *1sc into next st, 1dc into next st, 3tr into next st, 1dc into next st, rep from * to end, sl st to first sc.

Fasten off, leaving a 2½in-long end of yarn. Thread ends of yarn through 4ch circle.

Make 3 more flowers in the same way. Use ends of yarn to attach flowers to stem. Attach flowers at approx ⅜in intervals and bind stem with tape.

4 Primula

Use 2 colors, yellow and purple. Using yellow, ch5, sl st to first ch to form a circle.

1st round Working over approx 6in of craft wire work (1sc, 2dc) 5 times into circle, sl st to first sc. 15 sts.

Break off yellow and change to purple.

2nd round Ch 1, *1sc into next sc, (2dc, 1tr) into next dc, (1tr, 2dc) into next dc, rep from * 4 times more, sl st to first sc. 35 sts.

3rd round *1sc into next sc, 2dc into next st, (1dc, 1sc) into next st, (1sc,

1dc) into next st, sl st into next st, rep from * ending with sl st into first sc. Fasten off.

Insert one stamen into center of flower. Bind stamen and wire under flower.

Tape flower onto thick wire. Tape wire to form stem.

5 Lily

Using orange, ch6.

Base row 1dc into 4th ch from hook, 2dc into each of last 2ch. Turn. 6 sts.

1st row Ch 3, 1dc into base of 3ch, 2dc into next st, 1dc into each st to last 2 sts, 2dc into each of last 2 sts. Turn. 10 sts.

2nd and 3rd rows As 1st row. 18 sts.

4th row Ch 3, skip first st, 1dc into each st to end. Turn.

5th row As 4th row.

6th row Ch 3, skip first st, (work next 2dc tog) twice, 1dc into each st to last 5 sts, (work next 2dc tog) twice, 1dc into last st. Turn. 14 sts.

7th row Ch 3, skip first st, work next 2dc tog, 1dc into each st to last 3 sts, work next 2dc tog, 1dc into last st. Turn. 12 sts.

8th – 11th rows As 7th row. 4 sts.

12th row Ch 3, skip first st, work next 2dc tog, 1dc into last st. Fasten off.

Make 5 more petals in the same way. Bend craft wire to shape of petal, leaving 2 ends, each approx 2in. Working over wire, work one row of sc all around each petal. Place several large stamens in center of 3 petals. Arrange rem petals around first petals as shown. Twist petal wire and stamens together.

Tape flower onto thick wire. Tape wire to form stem.

Special technique — wired flowers

Working crochet flowers can be time-consuming, but very few special materials are needed.

Petals

Before you begin, examine an actual specimen. Work the petals as required, copying the natural flower by decreasing or increasing as necessary.

3 When all the petals have been wired, assemble the flower. Place the second petal next to the first, overlapping the edges as necessary. Bend the petals into the required shape — the wire makes them very pliable. Twist together the lengths of wire extending below the petals. Continue adding petals in this way, always twisting together the wire to hold the petals in position.

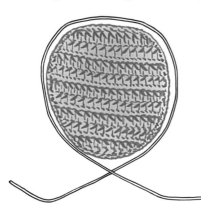

1 Unless the flowers are fairly small, they will retain their shape better if the petals are wired. Cut a piece of craft wire approximately 4in longer than the circumference of the petal. Bend the wire so that it surrounds the petal and extends in two 2in ends at the bottom.

Stems

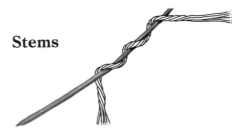

1 Cut a length of thick wire as required for the stem. Wind the twisted lengths of petal wire firmly around the top of the stem.

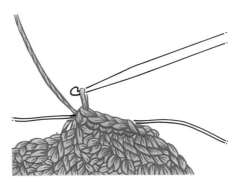

2 Rejoin the yarn to the lower edge of the petal and work a row of single crochet into the edge and enclosing the wire. Work the stitches closely together so that the wire is covered. Wire each petal in exactly the same way.

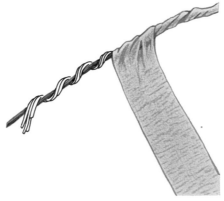

2 Wind florist's green tape tightly around the stem, beginning where the petals meet on the underside of the flower. Overlap the tape as you wind so that the stem wire is completely hidden.

Leaves

Large, unattached leaves — as on tulips — can be worked in much the same way as petals. Other flowers, however, have leaves which are attached to the stem.

1 When working a single attached leaf, make and wire it in the same way as a petal, twisting together the short lengths of uncovered wire. Unstemmed leaves can be attached as for the Iris leaf on page 134. For a stemmed leaf, work a few single crochets over the twisted wires to form the leaf stem. Twist the remaining wire around the main stem and bind the stem as above.

2 When working a leaf spray, work the individual leaves, each having a short stem, as above. Make a short stem from several lengths of craft wire twisted together. Twist the wires from the first leaf around the top of the leaf stem. Work single crochet very tightly over the wire to the position of the second leaf. Attach the second leaf as before. Continue in this way, leaving a length of uncovered wire. Use this to attach the spray to the main stem.

Utility bag

This versatile drawstring bag can be used for toiletries, makeup or even shoes if you line it with plastic. Increase its size and it becomes a useful beach holdall.

Size
Approx 14in × 16½in

Gauge
26 sts and 18 rows to 4in

Materials
8 oz fingering weight cotton yarn
Size B crochet hook
1yd each red and blue cord

To make
Ch 94.
Base row (RS) 1hdc into 3rd ch from hook, 1hdc into side of previous hdc, * skip next ch, 1hdc into next ch, 1hdc into side of previous hdc, rep from * to last 2ch, 1hdc into last ch. Turn.
1st row Ch 1, skip first st, 1sc into each st to end. Turn.
2nd row Ch 2 to count as first hdc, skip first st, *1hdc into next st, 1hdc into edge of previous hdc, skip next st, rep from * to turning ch, 1hdc into top of turning ch. Turn.
1st and 2nd rows form pat. Rep until work measures 16¼in.
End with a 2nd row of pat.
Work a second piece the same size.

To finish
Press each piece using a damp cloth and stretching work slightly but being careful not to pull it out of shape. Join the two pieces together by working a seam of single crochet around three sides, leaving the top open. Insert the hook through both layers and adjust the spacing of the stitches as necessary. Wrap one end of each cord with sticky tape to prevent fraying. Then thread the cord through the half double crochet rows at the top of the bag. Remove the tape, knot the ends of the cords; fray them out to make tassels. Damp and trim the ends of the tassels.

Lazy-days hammock

Crochet a super hammock and spend hot, lazy summer
days relaxing in it. We made ours in a strong white cotton
dyed a bright pink, and in attractive and durable Solomon's
knot stitch.

Size
Approx 86in long by 26in wide

Gauge
3 pats measure 4¼in on size F hook
with yarn used double
To save time, check your gauge.

Materials
Approx 3,200yds of a fingering weight cotton thread
Size F crochet hook
Two pieces of 1¼in-diameter bamboo, 21½in long
Two fiberglass rings, 3in in diameter

Note: The yarn is used double throughout. If you want the hammock in a color, dye the yarn before you crochet following the directions given.

Note: See steps 2–4 under Solomon's knot on page 159.

To make
1 Make a slip loop on the hook and then ch1. Work 1sc into the 1ch.
2 Extend loop on hook, drawing it out so that it is approximately ¾in in length. Wind yarn around hook and draw it through this loop.

Patterns and alternatives

3 Insert hook from right to left under the vertical thread that becomes the loop on the hook, wind yarn around the hook and draw it through so that there are 2 loops on the hook and all the extended strands of yarn are held together at the top.

4 Now wind the yarn around the hook and draw it through the 2 loops on hook to complete the first Solomon's knot st.

5 Repeat steps 2 to 4 36 times more, until you have 37 Solomon's sts in all.

6 Now work the pat row. Begin by working 6 ch, work 1 Solomon's st, sl st into first free knot before the 6 ch, *ch1, now work 2 Solomon's sts, skip next knot, sl st into the next knot, rep from * to end.
Turn.

7 Continue to work the pat row, but working last sl st into top of the ch, until work measures approx 86in at side edge. Fasten off.

8 Cut 4 lengths of yarn each about 100in long. Placing lengths of yarn along one side edge and using yarn double, work sc over ch and yarn to reinforce edge working 5 sc over the 6 ch and 1 sc into each row end. Fasten off. Leave about 6in of reinforcing yarn free at each end. Complete other side to match.

9 To attach bamboo, join 2 strands of yarn to first free knot at one end of hammock. Working over bamboo, work 1 sc into each free knot to end. Fasten off. Attach bamboo to other end of hammock in the same way.

10 Using the 6in of reinforcing yarn that was left free at each end, bind the ends of the bamboo and fasten with a square knot.

11 Cut 18 lengths of yarn each 55in long. Holding all the lengths together in a bunch with ends even, fold bunch in half. Slip folded end through ring and then pull ends through loop to knot

lengths to ring. Divide strands into 3 groups of 12 strands and braid together for 11½in. Tie knot at base. Divide unbraided strands in half, wrap ends over bamboo and knot tightly. Trim ends about 4in from knot to form tassel.

12 Repeat step 11 and work another braid from same ring and attach to other end of bamboo.

13 Repeat steps 11 and 12 at the other end of the hammock.

Basic skills

Most of the basic stitches and techniques you need to make the home accessories in *Crochet For a Beautiful Home* and alternatives of your own design are described here with clear directions and illustrations. Others are explained in the patterns.

STITCHES AND TECHNIQUES

Foundation chain (ch)

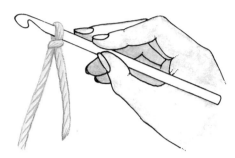

1 *Make a slip loop and place it over the hook. Hold the hook in your right hand as if you were holding a pencil.*

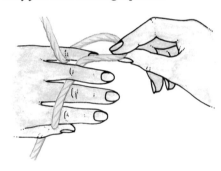

2 *Thread the yarn as shown between the fingers of the left hand so that it flows freely and evenly.*

3 *Take the yarn over the hook and draw it through the loop to make the first chain. After making a few chains, move your finger and thumb to just below the hook.*

Slip stitch (sl st)

1 *To work slip stitch along a foundation chain, insert the hook from front to back under the top two loops of the second chain from the hook. Take the yarn counterclockwise over the hook and draw it through the chain and the loop on the hook — one loop remains and one slip stitch has been worked. Continue in this way to the end.*

2 *Slip stitch is often used when shaping. When the required number of slip stitches has been worked, slip stitch into the next stitch, work the turning chain to count as the first stitch (here we show two for a half double fabric) and continue in pattern.*

3 *Slip stitch is also used when working in rounds to join the last stitch of the round to the first. After the last stitch has been worked, insert the hook into the top of the turning chain, which counts as the first stitch, and work a slip stitch.*

Single crochet (sc)

1 *To work the base row, skip the first of the foundation chains and insert the hook from front to back under the top two loops of the second chain from the hook. Take the yarn over the hook and draw through a loop — two loops on the hook.*

2 *Take the yarn over the hook and draw it through the two loops on the hook — one loop remains and one single crochet has been worked. Work one single crochet into the next and every foundation chain, then turn the work so that the hook is once more at the beginning.*

3 *To begin the next row, work one turning chain to count as the first stitch. Skip the last stitch of the previous row and work one single crochet into the second and every following stitch, working the last single crochet into the turning chain of the previous row. Repeat as often as desired to make a single crochet fabric.*

Half double crochet
(hdc)

1 *To work the base row, take the yarn over the hook and insert the hook from front to back under the top two loops of the third chain from the hook. Take the yarn over the hook and draw through a loop — three loops on the hook.*

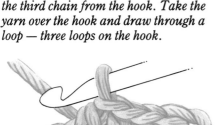

2 *Take the yarn over the hook and draw through all three loops — one loop remains and one half double has been worked. Take the yarn over the hook and work a half double as before into the next chain. Continue in this way to the last chain. Turn the work.*

3 *Work two chains to count as the first half double. Skip the first half double of the previous row and work into the second stitch.*

4 *Work one half double into each half double to the turning chain. Then work one half double into the top of the turning chain and turn.*

Double crochet (dc)

1 *Make a chain the length needed. Take the yarn counterclockwise over the hook. Skip the first three chains and insert the hook from front to back under the top two loops of the fourth chain from the hook. (The three chains skipped at the beginning are called the turning chain and should be counted as the first double crochet.)*

2 *Take the yarn counterclockwise over the hook and draw yarn through the chain — three loops on the hook.*

3 *Take the yarn counterclockwise over the hook. Draw the yarn through the first two loops on the hook — two loops remain on the hook.*

4 *Take the yarn counterclockwise over the hook. Draw the yarn through the remaining two loops on the hook — one double crochet has been worked and one loop only remains on the hook. Work one double crochet into the next and every foundation chain and then turn. Work three chains to count as the first double crochet in the next row and then work into the second stitch. At the end of the row, work one double crochet into the top of the turning chain.*

Triple crochet (tr)

1 *To work the base row, take the yarn counterclockwise over the hook twice and insert the hook from front to back under the top two loops of the fifth chain from the hook. Take the yarn once over the hook and draw through the first two loops of the hook — three loops remain on the hook.*

2 *Take the yarn over the hook and draw it through the first two loops on the hook — two loops remain. Take the yarn over the hook and draw it through the remaining two loops on the hook — one loop remains and one triple has been worked. Continue working triples in this way into the next and each chain to the end. Turn.*

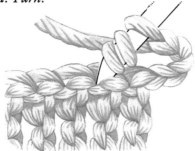

3 *At the beginning of the next and every following row, work four turning chains to count as the first triple and then insert hook into the second stitch. At the end of each row work the last triple into the top of the four turning chains.*

Double triple and triple triple (dtr and tr tr)

These long stitches are usually worked as part of an intricate stitch pattern.

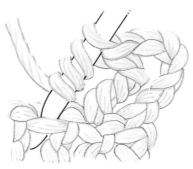

1 *Begin a double triple row with five turning chains. Yarn over hook three times and insert the hook into the next stitch. Yarn over hook and draw through a loop — five loops on hook. *Yarn over hook and draw through first two loops on hook*, repeat from * to * three more times until there is one loop left on the hook. One double triple has been completed.*

2 *Triple triple is worked in the same way except that each row begins with six turning chains and the yarn is wound over the hook four times. Insert the hook into the next stitch and work from * to * five times, when one loop will remain.*

Left-handed crochet

If you are left-handed in a right-handed world and would like to crochet, don't despair. With a little know-how, you can succeed.

Because right-handed people are in the majority, instructions and tools for most skills are designed with them in mind. Crochet patterns are no exception. It woud be costly in time, money and paper to print two sets of directions. Some left-handed people can learn right-handed crochet and, with practice, they become as proficient as the naturally right-handed. If you find this impossible, don't be discouraged; it is perfectly possible to crochet with the left hand.

Beginning

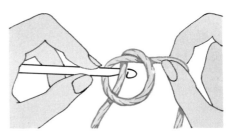

1 *Hold the hook lightly but firmly in your left hand. Make a slip knot on the hook and pull the short end of yarn to tighten the loop.*

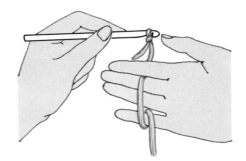

2 *To maintain even tension, wind the working yarn around the fingers of your right hand. Loop the yarn around your little finger, across your palm and behind your index finger. Pull the yarn gently so that it lies firmly around your fingers.*

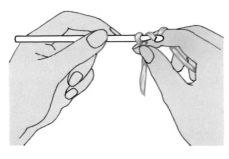

3 *To work the foundation chain, hold the short end of yarn in your right hand to secure the loop, take the hook under the taut working yarn and catch the yarn with the hook. Draw the yarn through the loop on the hook to form the first chain. Continue in this way.*

Basic stitches

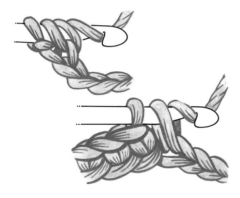

1 *Although left-handers crochet from left to right, the directions for basic stitches can usually be used by left- or right-handed people, though the illustrations are "right-handed." The illustrations above show the first two steps of single crochet as worked by a left-handed person.*

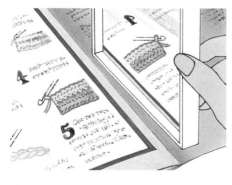

2 *The drawings in step 1 are the same as those on page 144, but they have been*

reversed and so are "left-handed." To reverse other illustrations in this book, simply hold a mirror at the side of the drawing at right angles to the page. The resulting mirror image will be left-handed.

Adapting patterns

Practice the basic crochet stitches until you are ready to tackle a pattern. For your first attempt choose something simple in a basic stitch.

Many crochet patterns, especially those for household accessories, do not have a left or right. When they do, read "left" for "right" and vice versa. With practice and common sense you will learn when to apply this rule.

Increasing

1 *To increase one stitch in a single crochet, half double or double crochet fabric, work two stitches into the top of one stitch in the previous row. Although increases are usually worked at the edges of the fabric, they can, if necessary, be worked into any stitch in the row.*

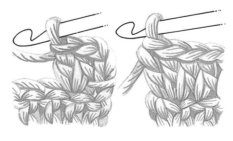

2 *It may be possible (depending on the pattern) to achieve a neater edge when increasing by working all the extra stitches one stitch in from each edge. At the beginning of the row work the turning chain, skip the first stitch and work two stitches into the next stitch; at the end of the row, work to within the*

last two stitches (including the turning chain) and then work two stitches into the next stitch and one stitch into the top of the turning chain.

3 *Occasionally it may be necessary to increase two or more stitches into one stitch of the previous row. To increase two stitches into one stitch, simply work three stitches all into one stitch (i.e. two increased stitches plus the original stitch).*

Decreasing

Decreases can be worked into any stitches, but are usually worked near the edges — if possible, one stitch in from the edge to ensure a neat finish. The principle is the same for single, half double and double crochet — two or more incomplete stitches are linked together into one stitch —, but the working methods differ.

1 *To decrease one single crochet stitch, insert the hook into the next stitch, yarn over hook and draw through a loop — two loops on the hook; insert the hook into the next stitch, yarn over hook and draw through a loop — three loops on the hook; yarn over hook and draw through all three loops — one single crochet decreased.*

2 *To decrease one half double stitch, take the yarn over the hook, insert the hook into the next stitch, yarn over hook and draw through a loop — three loops on the hook; yarn over hook, insert the hook into the next stitch and work as before until five loops remain; yarn over hook and draw through all five loops — one half double decreased.*

3 *To decrease one double, take the yarn over the hook, insert the hook into the next stitch, yarn over hook and draw through a loop — three loops on the hook; yarn over hook and draw through the first two loops — two loops on the hook. Work the next stitch as before until three loops remain, yarn over hook and draw through all three loops — one double crochet decreased.*

Fastening off

Work the last stitch of the last row in the usual way. Cut the yarn to approximately 4in. Take the yarn around the hook and draw through the loop on the hook to fasten off.

Joining in new yarn

Always join new yarn at the end of a row. Insert hook into turning chain, yarn over hook and draw through a loop — two loops on hook. Cut off old yarn to 4in. Complete stitch using the new yarn.

Splicing yarn

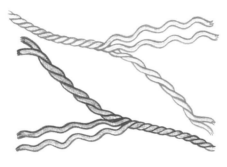

1 *When working rounds in crochet, it may be necessary to join yarns in the middle of a round. To make an invisible join you can splice the two ends of yarn together. Unravel the ends of each yarn, shown here in different colors for clarity.*

2 *Cut away one or two strands, depending on the thickness of the yarn, from each of the ends so that the two ends are of equal thickness.*

3 *Overlay the two ends from opposite directions and twist them firmly together. The twisted ends should be the same thickness as the original yarn. Work carefully with the new yarn; trim odd ends after the yarn has been securely introduced.*

Using two colors

1 *To change colors on any crochet fabric, work the stitch (double crochet shown above) as usual until there are two loops on the hook. Drop the old color and draw the new through two loops on the hook.*

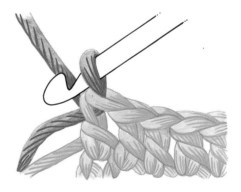

2 *When working in stripes, change color as in step 1 on the last stitch of a row, drawing the new color through the last two loops on the hook. Work the turning chain in the new color.*

3 *Use separate balls of yarn when working large areas in one color. However, when working only a few stitches in each color, carry the color not in use loosely on the wrong side at the base of the row, working over it with the other color.*

SIMPLE STITCH VARIATIONS

Interesting effects can be produced by varying slightly the method of working basic stitches. These variations are shown using double crochet stitches, but they could be used with most of the basic stitches.

Note: Unless the pattern states otherwise, begin a row with a turning chain to count as the first stitch and end a row by working into the top of the turning chain.

Working around the stem

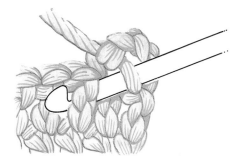

1 *To work a double crochet from the front — known as "1dc front" — around the stem of a stitch, take the yarn*

over the hook, and insert the hook from front to back into the space between two stitches. Bring the hook to the front of the work between the second and the next stitch. Complete the stitch in the normal way.

2 *Work a double crochet from the back — known as "1dc back" — around the stem of a stitch in the same way, but insert the hook between stitches from back to front and then from front to back.*

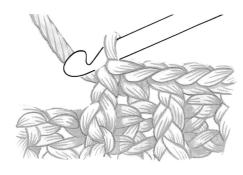

3 *A neat crochet rib pattern can be formed by working double crochets around the stem from the front and back alternately along the row.*

Working between stitches

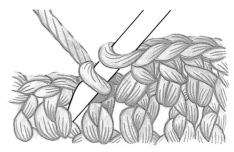

Take the yarn around the hook and insert the hook from front to back into the space between two stitches beneath

the small connecting loop at the top of the stitch. Complete the stitch in the usual way.

Working into a single loop

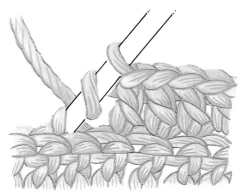

1 *To work a double crochet into the back loop of a stitch, take the yarn over the hook and insert the hook into the back loop of the two loops lying at the top of the stitch. Complete the stitch in the usual way.*

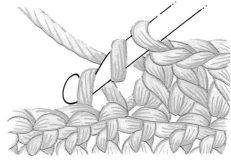

2 *A double crochet worked into the front loop of a stitch is formed in the same way, except that the hook is inserted into the front loop of the two loops lying at the top of the stitch.*

ROUNDS

Many types of squares in crochet, including granny squares, are worked in rounds.

Working rounds

1 *Make a small number of chains — usually between four and six — and join them into a circle with a slip stitch. Insert hook in first chain, yarn over hook, and draw through chain and through loop on hook.*

2 *On the first round, work four groups of double crochet stitches into the circle, separating the groups with chains. Fasten off.*

3 *To begin the next round, join the new*

color to the next chain space and work three chains to count as the first double. On this and following rounds work two groups of doubles into each corner and one group of doubles into each chain space along the sides, separating the groups with chain spaces.

Working an open center

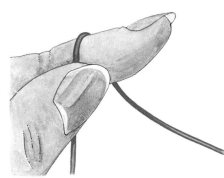

1 *Some rounds have a large, open center. This is sometimes formed from a fairly large circle of chains. The method shown here produces a neater center. Hold the yarn (about 4in from the cut end) over the little finger of your left hand. Hold the ball of yarn in your right hand.*

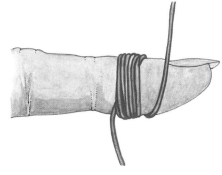

2 *Wind the yarn from the ball 20 times around the tip of your little finger. Cover the short end as you wind to secure it and wind firmly but not too tightly so that the resulting circle can be removed easily from your finger.*

3 *Carefully remove the yarn circle from your finger. Then, holding circle and working yarn in your left hand, use a hook of the required size to work a slip stitch into the circle to prevent it unwinding.*
Continue the round as given in the pattern.

Note: When using thicker yarn, wind the yarn fewer times around your little finger.

Working a closed center

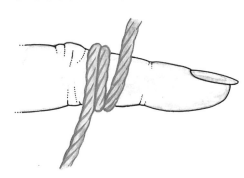

1 *The usual method for beginning a round by making a few chains and joining them with a slip stitch produces a hole at the center. This can sometimes be avoided by working the first round into a circle of yarn which can be closed when the round is finished. Leaving a long end, wind the yarn twice around the index finger to form a circle.*

rounds, omit the chain that is normal when working rounds of single crochet.

2 Remove the yarn circle from your finger and hold it tightly to keep it together. Work the turning chain into the circle. Continuing to hold the circle, work the remainder of the first round. Pull the long end slightly to close the circle if it is too large for the first round.

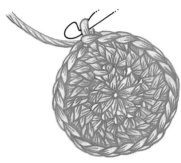

2 At the end of each round, do not join the first and last stitch with slip stitch as usual, but simply begin the next round by working one single crochet into the first stitch of the round.

3 Complete the round in the usual way and fasten off. Pull the long end at the center to close the hole. You may prefer to use this method of beginning whenever you work in the round. But some rounds will not lie flat if the center is closed, so you may not be able to close the center completely.

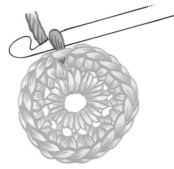

Continuous rounds

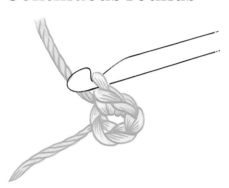

1 Many mats, rugs and other items are crocheted in continuous rounds. At the beginning of the first and following

3 To change color when working continuous rounds, work the last single crochet in the old color. Insert hook into first stitch of round and draw through new color. Continue in pattern, working into same place as join, using new color and working over end of old color.

FOUNDATIONS

Working a chainless base

1 A chainless base is simple to make, can be used when working in rows or in

rounds and is particularly useful when you want an elastic edge. Make four chains and work one double crochet into the fourth chain from the hook to form one large space.

2 Do not turn. Make three chains and work one double crochet into the space just formed to make a second space. Continue working spaces in this way until the base is the required length. Your pattern will tell you how many spaces are needed to work the first row or round.

3 To make the base circular, place it on a firm, flat surface and untwist it so that the right side of each double crochet stitch is uppermost. Bring the last space to meet the first so that the doubles lie on the inner edge of the circle. Slip stitch into the first space. Work the first round into the spaces.

Working an approximate foundation

1 *It can be difficult, especially when using fine yarn, to count accurately the number of stitches in the foundation chain. This problem can be avoided by working an approximate foundation chain. Work roughly the required number of chains plus about 25 more. Work the base row as given leaving a length of unworked chains.*

2 *Using sharp scissors, cut across the first chain worked, removing the slip knot with which you began. Discard the short piece of yarn now caught in the second foundation chain. Insert the point of the crochet hook into the loop at the end of the chain and draw through the loose length of yarn.*

3 *Continue drawing through yarn and undoing chains in this way until one loop remains. Do not draw through the yarn, but instead pull it firmly to tighten the last chain. The remaining end of yarn can now be used for seaming or can be darned into the edge of the work.*

Alternative foundations

Double chain

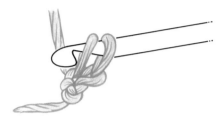

1 *A double chain forms a strong, neat, cabled edge and can also be used as a cord. Make two chains in the normal way. Insert the hook under the top loop of the second chain from the hook. Wind the yarn over the hook and draw through a loop.*

2 *Wind the yarn over the hook and draw through both loops on the hook to complete the first double chain. Insert the hook under the single loop lying to the left of the hook. Wind the yarn over the hook and draw through a loop.*

3 *Wind the yarn over the hook and draw through both loops on the hook to complete the second double chain. Continue in this way as required. When using the chain as a foundation, insert the hook under the two loops lying on one edge.*

Triple crochet chain

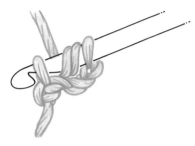

1 *The triple chain forms a fairly elastic edge for use with a plain fabric. Work four chains in the normal way. Wind the yarn twice over the hook and insert the hook into the fourth chain from the hook.*

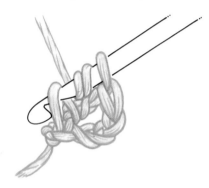

2 *Complete the triple crochet in the normal way. Wind the yarn twice over the hook and insert the hook into the single loop lying at the base of the previous triple. Complete the crochet triple in the normal way.*

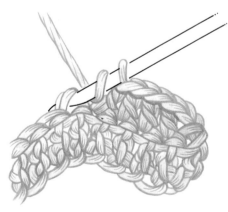

3 *Continue in this way as required. When the foundation is complete, turn, omit the base row and work the first row into the top two loops of each triple in the normal way.*

FINISHING TECHNIQUES

Working a shell edge

1 The shell chain forms an ideal foundation for lacy fabrics. Make five chains and work one double crochet into the fifth chain from the crochet hook.

2 Make three chains and work one double crochet into the last of the chains worked before the previous double.

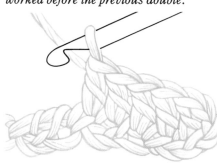

3 Repeat step 2 as required. When working the base row, work three stitches into the side of each double, inserting the hook under two loops each time. If the number of stitches required is not a multiple of three, work one extra or one fewer stitch into the last double, enclosing any surplus foundation when seaming the side edges.

Finishing an afghan

1 Before joining the pieces, darn in all ends of yarn. Place a clean sheet on the floor or a table and arrange the pieces in the correct order on it, making sure that the right sides of all the pieces face up.

2 Split lengths of left-over yarn in half and use two strands only when seaming. When the yarn has three plys or strands, discard the third strand. Join yarn on the wrong side of the first piece.

3 To join the pieces, place the first and second pieces together with wrong sides facing. Insert the needle under the top loop on the second piece which corresponds to the stitch on the first piece where you attached the yarn and pull through the yarn. Insert the needle under the next two corresponding top loops and pull through the yarn. Complete overcasting the seam in this way. Take the yarn to the wrong side and fasten off.

Working an invisible seam

1 This flat seam enables patterns to be matched easily and does not produce a hard ridge. With right sides up, place the pieces edge to edge, matching patterns.

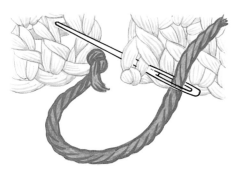

2 Using a matching yarn — shown above in a contrast color for clarity — and a blunt-ended wool needle, secure the yarn to one lower edge. Take the needle over to the other side edge and pass it under one stitch.

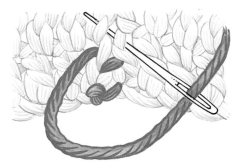

3 Take the needle back to the first side edge and under the next stitch. Pull the yarn through firmly to make the stitch invisible, but not so tightly that the fabric puckers. Continue catching one stitch on each edge, until the seam is complete.

Crochet seaming

1 *First edge the pieces with one row of single crochet, working one stitch into each stitch or row end. Turn corners either by working one chain at each corner or by working three single crochet stitches into each of the corner stitches.*

2 *To join, place the edged pieces* **together** *with* **wrong sides facing.** *Using the same yarn as that used for the edging, join the yarn at the beginning of the edges to be joined. Work one chain and skip the first stitch on the edging. Insert the hook under all four loops of the next stitch on both edgings and work one single crochet.*

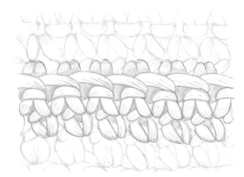

3 *Continue in this way, joining the edgings by working one single crochet into each pair of stitches on the edging. Joining pieces in this way produces a raised decorative seam which looks particularly attractive when worked in a color that contrasts with the main fabric.*

Stab stitch

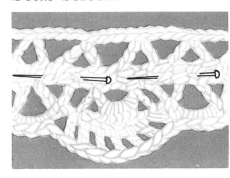

1 *Stab stitch is a method of invisibly attaching an edging to an article. After completing the edging, shape and pin it to the correct size. Lightly dampen and allow to dry. Place the edging with right side up on the front of the article and pin it in position.*

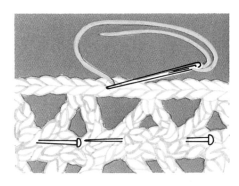

2 *Using a sharp sewing needle and thread to match the edging, begin with a small double backstitch on the back of the article. Bring the needle through all thicknesses to the front of the work and then, inserting the needle very slightly to the left, push it to the back of the work. Bring the needle back to the front about one-fourth inch to the left.*

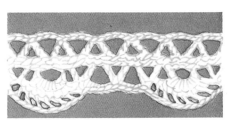

3 *Continue working stab stitch in this way to the end. Finish with a double backstitch.*

Working a crab stitch edging

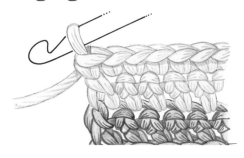

1 *Crab stitch is achieved by working single crochet from left to right instead of from right to left, usually on one or more foundation rows of single crochet, depending on how wide you would like the edging to be.*

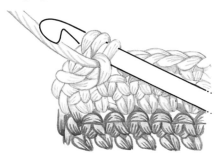

2 *Do not turn the work once the foundation rows have been completed. Keeping the yarn at left of work, work from left to right. Make one chain, then insert the hook from front to back into the next stitch. Hold the hook over the yarn before drawing yarn through from back to front.*

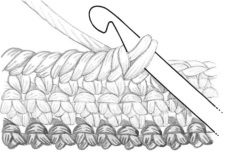

3 *Complete the single crochet in the usual way. Continue to work each stitch in the same way but working from left to right instead of from right to left to create the crab stitch effect.*

SPECIAL STITCH TECHNIQUES
Working a picot edging

1 *Join yarn and work two single crochet stiches and three chains for the picot. The number of chains can vary according to the size of the picot required.*

2 *To form the picot, work a slip stitch into the top of the last single crochet worked. This completes the picot.*

3 *Work three single crochets and a picot along edge of work.*

Working chevrons

1 *The zigzag effect of chevrons is produced by increasing and decreasing stitches alternately along the row. The zigzags point upwards where stitches have been increased and downwards where stitches have been decreased.*

2 *When working some chevron patterns, it can be difficult to keep the edges of the work straight. Patterns usually suggest, therefore, that you increase one stitch where the zigzag points down at the end of a row and decrease one stitch at the side edge where the zigzag points up.*

3 *To straighten top edges, work longer and longer stitches to the lowest point of the zigzag, working the longest stitch into the top of the decreased stitches, and then work shorter and shorter stitches to the highest point, working the shortest stitch into the center stitch of the increase.*

Working a berry stitch

1 *With the **wrong** side facing, work to the position of the berry stitch. Wind the yarn counterclockwise around the hook and insert the hook into the next stitch. Wind the yarn around the hook and draw through a loop **loosely**. Wind the yarn around the hook and draw through the first loop on the hook — three loops remain on the hook.*

2 *Wind the yarn around the hook and insert the hook into the same stitch as in step 1. Wind the yarn around the hook and draw through a loose loop as before — five loops on the hook. Wind the yarn around the hook and draw through the first four loops on the hook — two loops remain.*

3 *Draw the yarn through the remaining two loops — one loop remains and one berry stitch has been formed. When working an allover berry-stitch fabric, keep the work even by slip stitching into the next stitch and by working, on the following right-side row, a slip stitch into the top of each berry and a single crochet into the top of each slip stitch.*

Working clusters

1 *Clusters are formed by working a number of double crochet stitches together. Make an even number of chains. Yarn over hook, insert the hook into the fourth chain from the hook, yarn over hook and draw through the first two loops on the hook.*

2 *Working into the same chain, repeat step 1 until there are four loops on the hook, yarn over hook and draw through all four loops — one cluster worked. Work one chain, skip the next chain and work a cluster in the next chain. Continue in this way, working one cluster and one chain alternately.*

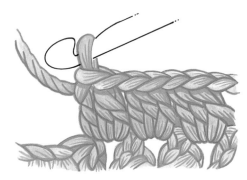

3 *Turn, work four turning chains and one cluster into the next one-chain space. Work one chain. Continue in this way to the end of the row, working one cluster into the space formed by the turning chain. To vary the size of the cluster work fewer or more doubles together.*

Triple crochet bobbles

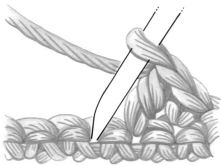

1 *Small bobbles can be worked on a single crochet fabric by bending triples in half. With the wrong side facing, work a triple crochet in the usual way. Work a single crochet into the next stitch, bending the triple crochet in half to form a small bobble on the front of the work. If the bobble seems flat after it has been bent in half, push it through to the right side of the work with the fingers.*

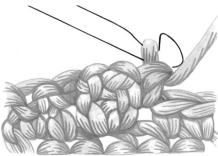

2 *Larger bobbles may be formed by working two or more triples into the next stitch, but leaving the last loop of each triple crochet stitch on the hook. Take the yarn over the hook and draw through all loops. Secure the bobbles as in step 1. (Wrong side shown above.)*

Double crochet bobbles

1 *Large bobbles or popcorn stitches can be worked by drawing double crochet stitches together. Work five doubles as usual into the next stitch. Remove the loop from the hook and insert the hook into the top of the first of the five doubles. Put the loop back on to the hook and draw it through the first double to form the bobble.*

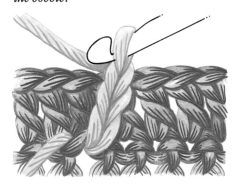

2 *Work large bobbles in another color or yarn after the main fabric has been completed. With right side facing, insert the hook into the free loop at the top of a stitch. Work three chains and four double crochets into the free loop. Complete the bobble as in step 1 and fasten off.*

Surface slip stitch

1 Use either one or two strands of yarn depending on how prominent you want the decoration to be. Hold the yarn at the back (wrong side) of the work and insert the hook from front to back into the foundation chain and draw through a loop to the front.

2 Insert the hook from front to back into the first row. Wind the yarn over the hook and draw through a loop to the front of the work to form the first slip stitch and to secure the yarn firmly.

3 Continue in this way up the fabric. You can either work a straight line or zigzags or curves. Your directions will tell you to work into, for example, ''one row above one stitch to the right'' or the pattern will be charted (see below).

Lacets

Lacets are two-row patterns, formed from a combination of V-shaped *lacets* and chain *bars*.

1 Patterns may be formed entirely from lacets, but often they are combined with filet spaces and blocks; in this case filet charts are used. The symbols are given in the diagram above, showing the number of chains in the lacet and bar.

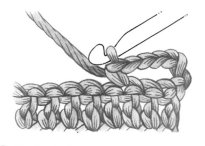

2 Begin the lacet row. Make six chains to count as the first double crochet and three chains. Skip the first three sts and work one single crochet into the next stitch. Chain three, skip the next two stitches and work one double crochet into next stitch.

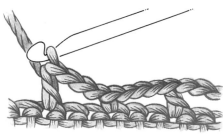

3 Chain three, skip the next two sts and work one sc into the next st. Chain three, skip the next two sts and work one dc into the next st. This step forms the lacet and is repeated to the end.

4 Work the bar on the next row. Begin with eight chains to count as the first double crochet and five chains. Skip the first double and work one double into the next double.* Chain five to form the next bar and work one double into the next double. Repeat from *.

5 To work a lacet over a bar, work the double crochets into the doubles of the bar row and work the single crochet into the third of five chains of each bar.

157

Loop stitches

There are three basic methods of making single or multiple loops.

Single loops

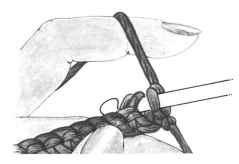

1 *Begin with a row of single crochet worked in the usual way. Turn, make one chain and skip the first stitch. * * Insert the hook from front to back into the next stitch. * Holding the yarn in the left hand as normal, extend the middle finger. The height of the finger governs the length of the loop.*

2 *Keeping the tension on the yarn with the little finger, take the yarn over the hook so that the hook is under and behind the middle finger of the left hand. Draw the yarn through the stitch — two loops on the hook.*

3 *Drop the loop and complete the single crochet stitch in the usual way, holding*

*the loop in place with the index finger of the left hand. Repeat from * * to the last stitch. Work one single crochet into the last stitch. Work the next row in sc. These two rows form loop pattern.*

Card loops

If you find it difficult to achieve regular loops by the previous method, you may prefer to work the loops over a strip of cardboard. The length of the loops is governed by the width of the strip. A ⅓ – 1¼in-wide strip is easiest, but a wider strip could be used.

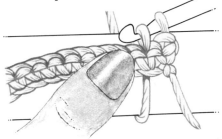

1 *Work to * as for single loops. Draw through a loop — two loops on the hook. Holding the strip behind the work, wind yarn around strip from front to back.*

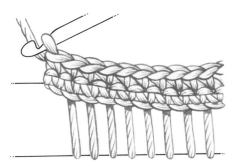

2 *Take the working yarn around the hook and draw it through the two loops on the hook. Continue working loops over the strip to the last stitch. Work one single crochet into the last stitch. Remove the strip. Turn and work one row of single crochet, to form the pattern.*

Multiple loops

Multiple loop stitches can be formed by winding the yarn around the fingers of the left hand. Steps 1 to 3 show how to work a double-looped fabric by winding the yarn twice around the fingers; for more loops, wind the yarn more times around the fingers.

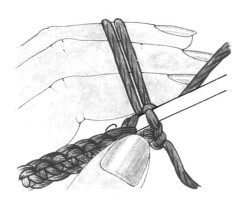

1 *Work to * as for single loops. Wind the yarn from front to back twice around the first three fingers of the left hand.*

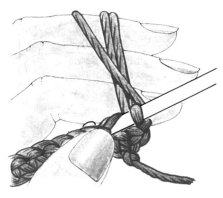

2 *Lay the yarn over the two strands of yarn as shown, winding it around the little finger to maintain the correct tension.*

3 *Insert the hook under all three strands of yarn and draw them through the stitch. Drop the loops and complete the single crochet. Continue in this way to the last stitch. Work one single crochet into the last stitch. Work the next row in single crochet. These two rows form pattern.*

Solomon's knot

Solomon's knot can be worked with or without a foundation chain, depending on whether a firm edge is needed. It can be difficult to work, so some practice is advisable.

1 *Make a slip loop on the hook and make one chain. Extend the loop on the hook to between ¼in and ½in depending on the yarn — the thicker the yarn, the longer the loop.*

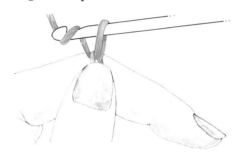

2 *Holding the extended loop between the thumb and index finger of the left hand, wind the yarn over the hook, extend the yarn to the same height as the loop and draw through a loop.*

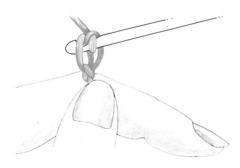

3 *Insert the hook from right to left under the vertical strand formed in making the loop in step 2. Yarn over hook and draw through a loop.*

4 *Wind the yarn over the hook and draw through both loops to complete the first knot. Continue in this way ending with a multiple of two knots plus two.*

5 *To begin the next row, insert the hook into the fifth knot from the hook and work a single crochet in the usual way. Always work into the center of each knot to ensure that they are joined firmly.*

6 *Work two more knots, skip the next knot and work a single crochet into the center of the next knot. Continue in this way working the last single crochet into the chain worked in step 1. Turn.*

7 *Begin every following row with three knots, then work a single crochet into next knot left unworked in the previous row. Make two knots; work one single*

crochet into the next unworked knot. Continue in this way working the last single crochet into next unworked knot.

Working into a chain

1 *To work a Solomon's knot fabric with a firm edge, begin with a multiple of five chains. Extend the loop on the hook and work one knot. Slip stitch into the tenth chain from the hook.*

2 *Make one chain and work two knots. Skip the next four foundation chains and slip stitch into the next chain. Continue in this way to the end, working the last slip stitch into the last chain. Turn.*

3 *Begin every following row with six chains and one knot. Work a single crochet into the next unworked knot of the previous row.*

4 *Work two knots and then a single crochet into the next unworked knot. Continue in this way, working the final single crochet into the turning chain of the previous row.*

Making a crochet cord

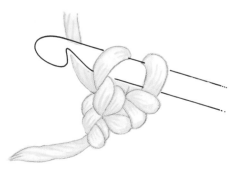

1 *Start with two chains. Hold the chain between finger and thumb of left hand and work one single crochet into second chain from hook. Turn the work so that foundation chain is at top. Insert hook into back loop and work one single crochet into foundation loop of second chain made at beginning.*

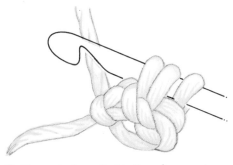

2 *Turn chain so that bottom is now at top next to hook and insert hook into the two loops at the side of the chain.*

3 *Take yarn over and through two loops on hook. Yarn over hook and through remaining two loops to make a twisted stitch. Turning stitches in this way produces a twisted cord.*

IRISH CROCHET

Formed by combining a simple or a picot mesh with elaborate motifs, Irish crochet is generally worked in fine cotton. Today, motifs are usually sewn on the mesh. Traditionally the motifs were made first, laid out and joined with picot mesh.

Working over a cord

To give a raised effect, Irish motifs — which are usually worked in single crochet — may be worked over a cord. Use as a cord either three or four strands of cotton thread twisted together or a thicker cotton thread in the same color. When the motif is completed, cut off the cord close to the stitches.

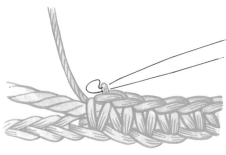

1 *Having worked the foundation chain, hold the cord at the back of the work in the left hand. Work into the chain and over the cord at the same time.*

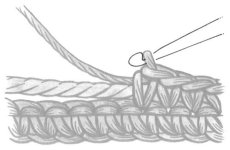

2 *At the end of the row, turn and work the next row over the cord, holding the cord at the back of the work.*

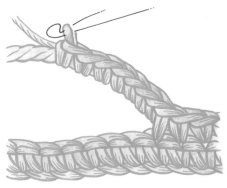

3 *To work over the cord alone, hold it away from the main body of the crochet, and work along the cord, pushing the stitches together to cover the cord.*

Seaming lace fabrics

Do not press Irish or any other crochet lace, but pin out the work to the correct size and lightly dampen it. Allow it to dry naturally.

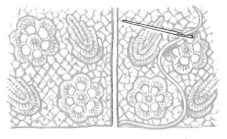

1 *With right sides up, place the pieces edge to edge as shown. Secure a matching thread to the lower corner of the RH piece.*

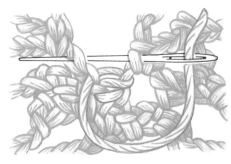

2 *Insert the needle under one thread on the left-hand edge, insert the needle under one thread on the right-hand edge. Continue in this way, pulling the thread tight so that the seam is invisible, but not so tight that the work puckers.*

FILET CROCHET

Filet charts

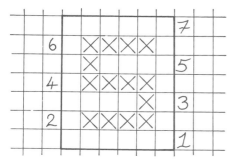

1 *Filet crochet is usually worked by following graphed charts, in which* **blocks** *of double crochets and chain* **spaces** *are shown as crosses and blank squares respectively. In the chart above, each blank square represents a two-chain space plus a connecting double crochet, while each cross represents two doubles plus a connecting double.*

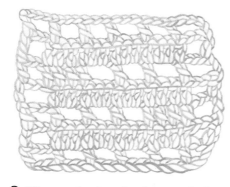

2 *The sample above has been worked following the chart in step 1. Read the odd-numbered rows from right to left; even-numbered rows from left to right.*

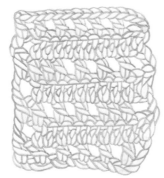

3 *Sometimes filet patterns are worked*

so that each space is formed from one chain plus a connecting double crochet and each block is formed from one double plus one connecting double. The same filet charts can be used. The sample above has been worked from the chart in step 1.

Mesh background

1 *Make a multiple of three chains plus two extra. Work one double crochet into the eighth chain from the hook. * Make two chains. Skip the next two foundation chains and work one double into the next foundation chain. Continue from * to the last foundation chain.*

2 *On the following rows, begin by working five chains to count as the first double crochet and two-chain space. Work one double into the next double. * Work two chains and then one double into next double. Continue from * to end, working last double into turning chain.*

Beginning with a block

1 *To begin a piece of filet with a block of*

double crochets, make enough foundation chains for the spaces and blocks on the first row. Work two more chains and then work one double into the fourth chain from the hook; the first three chains count as the first double crochet. Complete the first block by working one double into each of the next two foundation chains.

2 *On following rows, to begin with a block work three chains to count as the first double. Skip the first double and work one double into each of the next three doubles.*

Working a block above a space

Work one double crochet into the next connecting double. Then work two doubles into the space, followed by one double into the next connecting double.

Working a space above a block

Work one double into the next connecting double. Work two chains, skip the next two doubles and work one double into the next double.

TUFTED PATTERNS

Tufted fabrics greatly resemble candlewick and are ideal for bedspreads, pillows and blankets.

Extended single crochet

1 *This variation of single crochet is easy to work and is usually abbreviated as "exsc" in pattern directions. Begin with a length of chain in the usual way. Insert the hook into the third chain from the hook. Take the yarn over the crochet hook.*

2 *Draw a loop through the chain so that there are two loops on the hook. Take the yarn over the hook and draw through the first loop only on the hook — two loops on the hook. Take the yarn over the hook and draw through both loops on the hook to complete the first extended single crochet.*

3 *Insert the hook into the next stitch and take the yarn over the hook. Repeat steps 2 and 3 to complete the second extended single crochet. Continue in this way to the last chain and turn.*

4 *Because extended single crochet — as its name suggests — is taller than conventional single crochet, following rows begin with two chains to count as the first stitch instead of the single chain usually used when working single crochet. The last stitch on each row is therefore worked into the second of the two turning chains as shown.*

Making a tuft

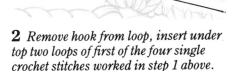

1 *Tufts are formed on the right side. Work in extended single crochet to first tuft. Work four extended single crochet stitches into next stitch.*

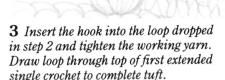

2 *Remove hook from loop, insert under top two loops of first of the four single crochet stitches worked in step 1 above.*

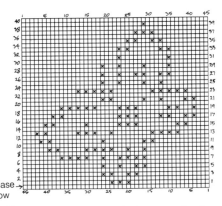

3 *Insert the hook into the loop dropped in step 2 and tighten the working yarn. Draw loop through top of first extended single crochet to complete tuft.*

Tufted-crochet charts

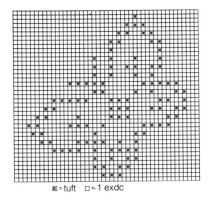

⊠ = tuft   □ = 1 exdc

1 *Most tufted-crochet designs are worked from a chart in which each blank square represents one extended single crochet and each cross represents a tuft formed from four extended single crochet stitches.*

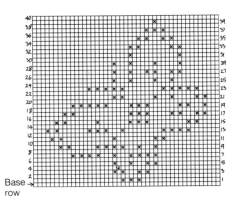

Base row →

2 *Tufted-crochet charts are numbered at the side edges in the same way as jacquard and filet charts. Even-numbered or right-side rows are worked from right to left and odd-numbered or wrong-side rows from left to right.*

Base row →

3 *On large charts, stitches can also be numbered. On lower edge stitches have been numbered from right to left to make stitch-counting easier on right-side rows. The top edge has been numbered from left to right to help on wrong-side rows.*

PADDED WORK

By padding or quilting with synthetic batting you can add texture and warmth to crochet.

Simple padding

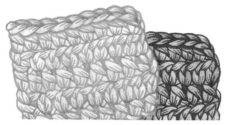

1 *Almost any shape can be padded, but rectangular pieces are best. Work two pieces of crochet with the same number of stitches and rows. The right-side piece can be decorative as long as the stitches used are closely textured to conceal the batting.*

2 *Use lightweight or medium-weight batting. Cut it ¼in smaller all around than the crochet. Place the batting on the wrong side of one piece of crochet and place the wrong side of the other piece on top. Pin through all three layers to hold them together.*

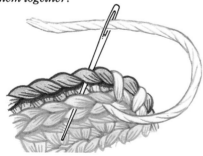

3 *Either join the pieces with single crochet or work a stitch-by-stitch overcast seam. For the latter, secure the yarn at*

the corner. Holding the two edges together, insert the needle under corresponding top single loops of both pieces and draw through the yarn.

4 *Continue in this way to the end. This method produces a neat, almost invisible seam.*

5 *To join the padded pieces, place them together with right sides facing. Use stitch-by-stitch overcasting as before, inserting the needle under the loops seamed in steps 3 and 4.*

Quilting

Quilting crochet is easier if you use your pattern as a guide — geometric designs are easiest. The wrong-side fabric is usually a lining fabric to reduce the thickness of the three layers. Allow more ease since quilting reduces the area of the crochet.

1 *Cut batting to the same size as the crochet. Cut out lining approximately*

½in larger all around than the crochet to provide a seam allowance. Place the batting on the wrong side of the lining and then place the wrong side of the crochet on top of the batting.

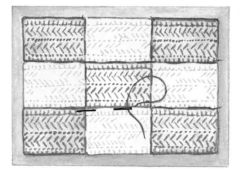

2 *Using a contrasting sewing thread, baste through all three layers along the quilting lines. Stitch along the quilting lines. Experiment to find the best stitch length and foot pressure. Remove the basting stitches.*

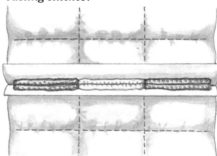

3 *To seam quilted crochet, place the quilted pieces together with right sides facing. Stitch approximately ⅝in from the edge catching the edge of the crochet. Trim the lining seam allowance on one side only.*

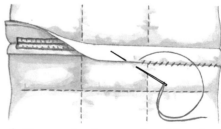

4 *Turn under the raw edge of the other lining seam allowance and slipstitch it to the lining on the other side to hide the raw edges. Bind the outer raw edges either with strips of crochet or with bias strips of lining fabric.*

FABRIC WORK

Use strips of fabric as "thread" for crochet. It is quite possible to mix weights and types of cloth. Before beginning, sort the fabric into dark-, light- and medium-colored groups.

Preparing the strips

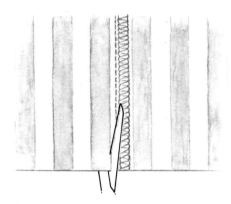

1 *If you are using old clothes, wash and iron them first. Cut the garment apart close to the seams. Don't waste time trying to rip out the seams since the fabric there is likely to be heavily creased and weakened by stitching.*

2 *The strips are generally cut on the bias since this provides strong strips that are less likely to fray. The extra strength gained by cutting on the bias is necessary for articles likely to receive hard wear. To find the true bias, fold the fabric so that the horizontal grain is parallel to the vertical grain. Mark the bias using tailor's chalk.*

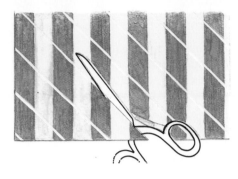

3 *Open out the fabric and, using a ruler and tailor's chalk, mark ⅝in-wide bias strips on the fabric. Then, using sharp dressmaker's scissors, cut out the strips. There is no need to overcast or finish the edges; the slightly frayed edges give an interesting "furry" appearance.*

Joining the strips

Choose one of the methods below to join the strips. As they are joined, wind the fabric into a ball.

1 *Make the joinings a feature of a garment — this method is not suitable for household accessories — by knotting the strips together with a square knot. As you crochet, push the knots through to the right side.*

2 *If the crochet will not receive hard wear and you prefer an invisible join, trim the ends of the old and new strips*

diagonally. Overlap the strips by about 3in and work with the double thickness until the new strip is secured.

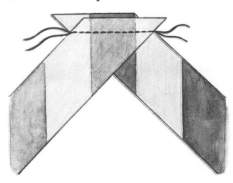

3 *For a strong join, overlap the strips, cut the edges to an angle and place them together as shown. Then machine stitch the two strips together approximately ¼in from the edges. Machine stitching makes the strongest possible join.*

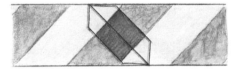

4 *Trim the loose threads. Press open the seam and trim the corners as shown to make a neat join. Each join should be treated similarly throughout the work.*

Working with fabric

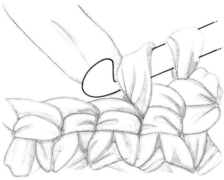

In general, crochet with fabric as you would with yarn, beginning and fastening off in the usual way. The fabric strips will naturally fold as you crochet. Don't try to open them out — the folds add to the texture and strength of the finished crochet as well as to its visual effect.

Index

Index

Picture credits